12-20-72

Psychoanalysis in Our Time

Psychoanalysis in Our Time

ESSAYS

Stefi Pedersen

Translated by Victoria Schultz

THE BOBBS-MERRILL COMPANY, INC.

INDIANAPOLIS   NEW YORK

First printed in Sweden in 1968 under the title
Psykoanalys i var tid: Fortroendekris och alienation
by P.A. Norstedt and Söner, Stockholm, Sweden
© Stefi Pedersen 1968
Translated into Norwegian: Psykoanalyse i var tid. Aschehongs Forlag,
Olso 1970, Norway.

The Bobbs-Merrill Company, Inc.
Indianapolis · New York
Copyright © 1973 by the Bobbs-Merrill Company, Inc.
All rights reserved
Library of Congress Catalogue Card Number 70-173220
Designed by Jack Jaget
Manufactured in the United States of America

Contents

C801182

1. REFUGEES

"For here we have no continuing city but we seek one to come."
Brahms: *A German Requiem*

Flight and Reality:
Some Mental Hygienic
Observations on Emigration

O NE WINTER DAY during World War II we walked over the mountain to Sweden. Below us lay the Norwegian countryside, lit by the sun and clear in the ice-cold air. It already seemed so far away down there. And after a time our life there would seem equally remote—the day when we would look back on it. In front of us were the dark ridges. It was there Sweden began. We were in no-man's-land, with a longing to return and the new land before us. We made a fire and sat down on some chopped-down tree trunks around it. There were also some children with us. It was not the first time they had found themselves escaping. Five years earlier they had come up from Austria.

I felt the children's small knapsacks, which now, after the trek, had very little food in them. When I opened one of the knapsacks to see what was left, I found among the old remains of paper and bread crumbs a small silver star, the sort that people often hang on their Christmas tree. I picked it up in surprise. At the same time I sensed that the child who owned it suddenly was staring at me a little embarrassed, as if I had discovered some secret. I put back the star without saying anything. But in one bag after another I found the cheap Christmas tree decoration again and again, stars and bells of cardboard, covered with silver glitter, that these children, raised in the Jewish faith, had taken with them from Norway. Otherwise they owned nothing except what they wore on their backs.

What did these little trophies mean to these children who were not used to celebrating Christmas with sparkling Christmas tree and festivities? It might not be farfetched to assume that the small paper objects had been taken along on the trip as symbols of everything they'd had to leave behind them in the country that had so hospitably welcomed them. It was as if by magic they had tried to cast a spell on the anguish they felt in the presence of the new and the unknown by taking with them an object from a happy past. When they had to venture out into no-man's-land, where every flight is a journey out into nothing, the cheap little paper stars assuaged their loneliness and feeling of impotence. It was the only thing they could attach their love and longing to, when they had been deprived of all other tokens of love. Perhaps—it occurred to me—even the star of Bethlehem was nothing more than a humble stable lantern radiating peace and protection upon the Jewish people (back in the good old days).

But not only the children seemed to have attached themselves to such trophies. That same evening, when we had a roof over our heads and friendly Swedish voices around us, a young Norwegian woman who had walked all the way over the mountain by herself arrived. She said that she had been given a half hour's notice to pack the bare essentials. The knapsack could not be too heavy. She knew she had several days of traveling ahead of her. Now she was unpacking: some dirty clothes that she had not had the time to wash, a rolled-up skirt, a pair of shoes—and a music box. She had gotten it from someone she had been in love with. It was a heavy brass box that played charming, tinkling melodies when it was opened. "Ub immer Treu und Redlichkeit," the music box sang in the refugee barracks. "Well, I had to take something nice with me since I was going to leave," she said apologetically.

The Danish actor Jacob Texière said in an interview that the only thing he had managed to take with him across the sound between Denmark and Sweden was a little snuffbox that had belonged to Hans Christian Andersen. It was odd to see the bags and the knapsacks among these refugees. Next to the absolute necessities you would find rather peculiar objects that seemed completely out of place in the poor and simple surroundings. I particularly remember a small suitcase with a few sportsclothes in it—and a pair of gold high-heeled shoes.

None of these objects was related in any rational way to the situation during the flight. They are evidence of efforts to adjust in a world that we cannot regard as normal and in which our usual mechanisms for adjustment no longer suffice. Often in such situations of utter powerlessness we unconsciously fall back on the use of magic as a means to master the world around us. The straws people clutch at when they're running away acquire their symbolic meaning from the fact that they represent their whole life. They attach themselves to dead objects and surround these objects with the tenderness and warmth they are prevented from giving to living people. In this way these symbols express the last remnant of a positive outlook on a reality that threatens to annihilate and exterminate them. In the face of the blunt fact that "you can't take it with you" is the life-sustaining, magical gesture of these meager objects: "I took it with me anyway!"

The double function of the symbols appears unambiguous here; on the one hand, they serve to deny the real danger that exists by magically manifesting the opposite. But at the same time, the denial of reality is the only weapon with which to overcome the threat of danger posed by precisely this denied reality.

There are also attempts at adjustment that at first seem to be of a purely negative nature. For the most part these efforts are lacking in this convincing, magic gesture. At first glance they do not seem like attempts at adjustment at all. In fact, I have been able to observe a pronounced form of depersonalization among people who have escaped. There was a woman who, during the flight itself, had not shown any signs of anxiety or depression. All that could be observed was a certain hardness, an insensitivity and a terseness that were the opposite of her usual manner. When she came to Stockholm, things worked out pretty well for her without much trouble. She began to view the circumstances she had very much feared with a certain relief. But at the same time, as the external situation became somewhat stable, she noticed that her memory failed her now and then. It was as if great portions of her life had been blotted out.

On one occasion, when she was asked her profession, she was not able to say what it was. She stared helplessly at the questioner and said: "I don't know!" During a police interrogation some time later it became apparent that she had "forgotten" the year and date of her birth. The names of close friends or of books and authors she liked had also vanished. Furthermore, she had the feeling that she would be obliged to begin all over again, from the very beginning. In connection with her loss of memory, there was some uncertainty both in the process of thinking itself and in her choice of words. During this time she was troublesome to the people around her; to questions that had to be answered clearly and decisively, she gave vague, generalized answers. In discussions she came up with evasive, general expressions far from the special consideration of the situation at hand.

That condition lasted several weeks, until a special experience contributed to bringing about a substantial change.

One evening she heard the news on the radio about the mass execution of deported Jews in Poland. She immediately had a violent anxiety attack, with dizziness, palpitation of the heart and a tendency to black out. This lasted several hours. During the following days she was preoccupied with thoughts of suicide. She felt no actual urge to take her own life. But rather coldly she considered that this possibility always was at hand, even though her environmental situation in Sweden was more secure than it had been at any point during the past three years. Perhaps it was this same environmental security in life that encouraged her to act out her anxiety and suicidal tendencies. The thoughts of suicide persisted for some weeks. They ended with a dream in which the rotating neon sign of Nordiska

Kompaniet (NK)* became a symbol of her new attitude toward Sweden.[1] She no longer regarded it only as an unknown, foreign country but also as a place where she could continue living in ways she considered somewhat worthy of human beings. In a sense one can say that in her unconscious she had rediscovered the political concept of Nordic unity. Thereby the continuity between her earlier life and way of thinking and her existence as an emigrant was reestablished. As a result of this, her amnesia disappeared.

Indeed it would not be difficult to perceive this kind of amnesia as a form of depersonalization. Through her loss of memory she was deprived of her past and had become unable to project into the future, for she lacked the necessary background in experience. She herself did not actually exist. There was only an automatically reacting outer shell. It was as if she were in no-man's-land. The world had been destroyed.

Such feelings of catastrophe, when the whole world collapses and a person no longer knows where and who he is, occur often at the onset of mental illness. The Danish writer H. C. Branner has described them in a little short story called *"Trommene"* ("The Drums"). A man who is on the verge of mental illness writes to a woman with whom he is in love and tells her about his anxiety in having forgotten who he really was. In his despair, he takes out old newspaper clippings on which his name and picture were printed.

Maybe it was only to see my picture and my name in print. To see that I really existed. You may not believe it, but at that stage the anxiety was already so strong in me that I was not quite sure I existed. I tried to read what the papers had written about me, but I couldn't keep my eyes on it, the letters got so blurry. When I closed one eye and took my magnifying glass, I could see a circular figure rise up out of the fog and grow sharp and clear. But I didn't recognize the words or know what they meant. I said to myself that it would only take a moment, it was merely a little mechanism that had suddenly got snarled. I only had to sit quiet for a moment. I took a pencil to help myself along, I wanted

---

*Nordic Company is the largest department store in Stockholm.

to write a word that I knew. But which word? My name! I closed my eyes and I tried to see my name in front of me. I couldn't see it. I tried to say my name to myself. I couldn't say it. I had forgotten it. I didn't have any name.

But the reason for this sense of depersonalization and destruction of the world—which are two aspects of the same process—is quite different in the above-mentioned case. The man who is writing the letter is becoming mentally ill. He tries to defend himself against anxiety over a world which is so singularly transformed, which has become so distant and strange, because crucial changes have occurred within his own self. In the other case, on the contrary, the external world really has broken down.

A reality that poses a threat of deportation back to Poland is unfathomable. It's not life, but neither is it death—yet. It is inconceivable. There is no possibility of comprehending it. And what one cannot understand, one cannot adapt oneself to. Even the most reality-bound person would lack adequate forms of reaction if he were to vegetate in the hold of a dark gray warship, where women and children were thrown one on top of another like old rags, to come to a country where he was to "begin a completely new life," as the Swedish Department of Cultural Affairs expressed it to a syndicated-news correspondent. As a result of this same incomprehensibility, one has a feeling of not being able to express it in print either. A person lacks words in no-man's-land. Probably no one has expressed this dumbness better than Bertil Malmberg in an article on the Jewish children:

> To call this event "terrible," "appalling," or "disgusting," in short, to characterize it is to deprive it of some of its incomparability, to make it bearable at least for the mind, that is blasphemous, the unintentional infringement on all those for whom the nameless is and remains nameless and impossible to name.

In such a situation, which represents a complete break with what we of the European civilization call "life," this woman reacted in a completely affectless way.

All of her mental activity became restricted and concentrated on tasks most closely associated with her flight. This state, resembling a traumatic paralysis, was experienced as ghastly by the woman herself. As she walked over the mountain to Sweden, she said constantly to herself: "Now you're leaving everything you like, now you're heading toward nothing." But at the same time she felt that she was incapable of experiencing this. While she walked the long path over the border, almost automatically her senses functioned with an alertness and precision they had never known before.

She took in everything as dispassionately and as accurately as a camera. The landscape and the people during the trip would remain unchanged, clear and alive for her all through the future. And one day—this she knew—she would take out the pictures and really experience them.

It would appear that in this case depersonalization served to avert the only reaction that would have had any meaning in a sober appraisal of the situation: suicide. But the fact that she forgot the year and the date of her birth (which can, of course, be seen as a symbolic suicide attempt) shows that suicidal impulses try to break forth when the situation has become safer.

On the other hand, the optimistic feature that was so apparent in the symbols is lacking. The depersonalization is no longer a correction of reality. Here reality is already in the process of being destroyed. But still—as paradoxical as it may sound—even here one can trace an attempt to take along that which is irretrievably lost. It has already been suggested by the concept (strange in itself) formulated on the trip over the mountain, "I'll remember it afterward," and the photographic exactness with which the pictures of this last trip had been printed. The comment that "I'll remember this afterward" meant that the experience of leave-taking and the sorrow over what was lost were too overwhelming. It would have demanded far too much strength.

In such a situation, when all her energy had to be used to make the escape, a realistic evaluation of the danger would have rendered her incapable of going through the struggle. The affect block was not enough. Her memory continued working and showed her with painful clarity in image after image all that she would no longer be able to see. The loss of memory stepped in to allay her sorrow.

Probably the remarkable thing about the behavior mechanisms I have sketched here is that they represent the only possibility of sustaining life and faith in this world in the face of danger which is so overwhelming and so unfathomable that rational ways of reacting no longer suffice. A full recognition of reality would have mobilized such great anxiety that it could have paralyzed the individual. Magical means of expression and a radical loss of memory of a happy time, attached to the country that was to be abandoned, turned out to be the only way to sustain life.

1945

Legal Abortion

A YOUNG POLISH woman of about twenty-five had succeeded in finding a place of refuge in Sweden. After she had lived there for a time she became pregnant and made inquiries about getting an abortion. Her history and her present circumstances were such that it was clear that she ought to be granted a legal abortion.

Her life story follows:

The patient grew up in an orthodox Jewish family and had a sister two years younger than herself. When she was five years old her father died. The mother took over the family business, and she managed to find the time to tend to it as well as her children and the household. The family life was harmonious. The patient was fond of her mother, whom she considered an exemplary person and a good friend as well.

She spent ten years in a girls' school. She liked the school, but it soon became obvious that her talent was for practical things, and she enjoyed helping with the housework. In 1938, some years after she finished school, she married a young medical student and acquired her own household. The first year of their marriage was happy until the great storm broke out across the country and took with it the quiet, friendly, undisturbed atmosphere of the patient's life.

After Germany declared war on Poland in 1939, the patient and her family no longer wanted to remain in the country. A few days after the war started, she fled to Russia with her husband, her mother and her sister. When winter came, they tried illegally to get across the border back into Poland to fetch some warm clothes. She suffered greatly from the cold and it was impossible to buy any clothes whatsoever in Russia.

Some distance ahead of the border between Russia and Poland, a Russian border patrolman arrested her and put her in jail. There she spent 14 days, after which she was freed. She tried again to cross the border and succeeded this time in reaching Warsaw, where she found some of the things they had left behind when they fled.

The winter of 1939–40 was unusually cold, which made it impossible for her and her husband to follow their original plan to cross the border back into Russia. They were forced to stay in Warsaw. In 1941 they were driven out of their apartment in the non-Jewish sector and sent to the ghetto. She was forced to work in a German uniform factory, and her husband was put to work repairing the streets. In 1942 she was sent on a "transport" to the gas chamber, from which she escaped at the last minute. By devious ways she succeeded in getting back to the ghetto, the only place where they were temporarily safe.

In 1943 the Germans set fire to the entire ghetto, but the patient and her husband survived. They both took part in the armed uprising of the Jews in 1944, which motivated the German troops to destroy the ghetto completely. After the destruction she and her husband literally went underground and for four months moved from one bunker to another. In August 1944 she was one of the nine survivors who succeeded in escaping (from of the ghetto) through the sewers.

From August 1944 to the spring of 1945 she remained hidden with several non-Jewish Polish families while her husband fought with the partisans along the Russian border. Early in 1945 she joined the alien's section of the organization Todt, using false papers. The danger of denunciation and lack of money made it impossible for her to stay any longer in Poland.

In April 1945 she was sent to Norway, where she met two Polish-Jewish girls whom she had previously known and who had likewise been smuggled into the labor organization with false papers.

After a short while the girls were recognized by a Polish SS man. The three of them were arrested, but the patient was released a few days later because there was no proof that she was Jewish. As she was afraid that the other girls would reveal her identity under the pressure of interrogation, she tried to leave the country. She came into contact with the Norwegian resistance and within 12 hours she was helped across the border into Sweden.

In Sweden she lived in modest circumstances from refugee-aid allotments and was isolated both mentally and physically. Her only thought was to get back to Poland and find her mother. She hoped her mother might be among the 150,000 Polish Jews who had fled to Russia during the war and who were then about to be repatriated. But she didn't really know whether her mother was still alive; she hadn't had any news of her in the last years and knew only that she had been sent to Arkangelsk in 1941. Hopes of finding her husband were even fainter, for she had heard nothing of him since he had joined the partisans in 1944.

In the meantime, in Sweden, she had become pregnant and admitted quite openly that she hadn't used any means of contraception as she didn't know where to get any and was afraid to ask. She then found out that she might run into difficulties in trying to get an abortion. She stated definitely that if she didn't, she would commit suicide. "I have seen so many dead people around me. I have gotten so used to death that it no longer scares me."

She felt in no way bound to the man she had been with and her only wish was to get back to Poland as soon as possible. She said that this was the only thing she had in her mind. "If I'm not able to see my mother again, I'll never be able to start living like a normal human being."

She claims to be the only woman to have survived the destruction of the Warsaw ghetto, which in 1941 had about 200,000 inhabitants. For people who have always lived in relatively secure and stable conditions, her story must seem almost incomprehensible, for however well we may imagine its terror, we cannot realize just what it was like to have lived in that way.

For this reason I am adding my complete notes of her first session with me. They consist mostly of a verbatim report of her own presentation.

The patient gave the impression of being a lively, temperamental and robust person. She was more like a chubby Viennese woman than a Polish Jew. Her movements were sure and rapid and she showed very little distrust in comparison to other refugees with similar backgrounds, so that it was easy to communicate with her.

Although she didn't speak German very well, she succeeded in giving a vivid description of her experiences, and when she lacked words, she used instead easily understandable expressive gestures.

During the conversation it became apparent that she had certain facial tics: she blinked with one eye and her mouth twitched. One got the impression of deep emotional instability. She would laugh loudly and triumphantly when she told of overcoming some danger and the next minute would burst into tears, demanding, "Why me? Why should I alone have survived?" A little later she would again interrupt her story and say bitterly and reproachfully, "But you don't believe me." When I tried to reassure her that I did believe her, she said aggressively, "But you don't have the imagination to realize what it all means." She didn't listen to my protesting explanation that whether I had the imagination or not, I was nevertheless interested in what she was saying, and simply said: "Oh well, I'll cut my story short." This, however, didn't prevent her from talking for four and a half hours without giving me a chance to make any comments or ask questions. Now and then she looked up at the clock and said, "Oh God! Is it so late?" but, indifferent to time, she continued to talk.

Her presentation was disjointed; often she got entangled in details, but she always managed to pick up the thread of her story. This story is both moving and truthful and totally focused on her own personal experiences. She makes no attempt to see her sufferings in an objective, social or political light.

The content of her story is approximately the following:

When the war came to Poland in 1939, neither she nor her husband wanted to remain in occupied Poland, and so they fled just as they were to the Russian-occupied zone and remained there until the winter. As a matter of fact, life wasn't bad there, but it was impossible to obtain clothing, and they suffered terribly from the cold. Finally, they could not bear it any longer and tried to return to Warsaw illegally. It was a cold winter with much snow. Just before reaching the frontier they were arrested by the Russians. The patient laughed in a good-natured way as she described the Russian prison. "We didn't get much food there, but they were quite nice and finally they let us go." Then they continued their trip and, at last, after many detours, they succeeded in reaching Warsaw. There they found the possessions they had left behind and attempted to return, illegally once again, to Russia. But when they heard that the border control was stricter and the snow several feet deep, making it impossible to avoid the highways, they abandoned their plans. The patient felt bad about this decision because she was very much attached to her mother, who had remained in Russia, and she had received no news from her.

She interrupted her story several times to say, always spontaneously and warmly, "My mother is my best friend. She always has been. I'm very fond of her. I could never have gone through all this if I hadn't been longing to see her again."

In November 1941 she and her husband were driven out of their apartment and sent to the ghetto. They could take only the bare essentials with them in a small suitcase. In the ghetto they had to live in a room with 12 other people. After only a few days, a typhoid epidemic broke out, for the sewage system was not working properly, and there was little to eat.

The ghetto was surrounded by a high wall, topped with

broken glass and guarded outside by SS men. Inside the ghetto as well there were SS soldiers, mainly Germans, Ukrainians and Lithuanians. One was known as the "Jew-eater." When he walked through the ghetto streets everyone ran away, because he shot every Jew he met, shouting at the same time that he wouldn't eat breakfast till he had killed 20 Jews. Often it was 50, sometimes 100.

The patient worked in a ghetto factory where German uniforms were made. Her husband had to go with the other young men to repair the railroad lines, which were outside the ghetto, and he was not permitted to go back into the ghetto in the evening. Together with the other young men, he slept in a cold, crowded barrack.

In 1942, just before Passover, there was a rumor in the ghetto that the SS men intended to prevent the Jews from celebrating their holiday. The evening before Passover, orders were received that 200,000 Jews, along with their children, were to gather in three narrow streets at five in the morning. The streets were crowded with people, who were hardly able to move. They tried to hide their children as well as they could because the SS had a special liking for shooting them or hitting them with their rifle butts. The Jews standing in the street had sewn the children into bags, packed them in suitcases or done their best to hide them under their coats. But the children betrayed themselves when they started crying and screaming and thus drew attention to themselves.

Two hundred thousand people stood in these three small streets for two whole days without anything to eat and without an opportunity to lie down. Then a group of soldiers arrived and made a selection, a process they called "segregation." Forty thousand young people, mainly men, were ordered to stay in the ghetto. The rest of the people were to be "resettled," as they called it.

The patient was among those who were to be resettled. She could not understand why she was chosen, because she was young and at that time still strong. She ran to one of the soldiers and clung to him, crying, "Must I go, too?" There was no answer, only a blow from a rifle butt.

The 160,000 chosen were transported in open freight cars to an unloading station from which small trains went directly to the gas chamber. When the trains arrived at the unloading station, they were unlinked, and the doors of the station were locked so no one could escape. There were corpses on the floor everywhere. If people tried to walk around the dead, the soldiers would grab them by the neck and force them to step on the bodies.

"Can you imagine what it's like to step on people?" the patient asked. "It's horrible. You're terror-stricken." She suddenly jumped up and started to step about with her feet. "It's like this, you have to do it this way," she yelled, suppressing her rage, and then started crying. Then she sat down and started mumbling to herself, "And there was so much blood and such a stench. I couldn't understand how the others were so apathetic. They only said, 'We have to die; there is nothing we can do about it.'"

The patient's reaction was quite different. She started sobbing and flailing her arms about, shouting that she wanted to live. She was obsessed with the thought of hiding somewhere and in that way avoiding extermination. Over and over again she saw the image of her mother before her, as if she were prompting her to save herself.

At first she ran about without any plans, shaking the doors of the unloading station, but they were locked and remained that way. Then she tried to crawl under the corpses in order to hide herself.

"You know, it was just like pulling a blanket over you," she said and reached for a tablecloth, pulling it over her head to demonstrate.

In this way she remained hidden for several hours, but the station became emptier and emptier, and there was the danger that she would be taken away with the bodies.

She crawled out again and suddenly had an ingenious idea.

Grotesquely enough, there was a medical post in the station with doctors and nurses who took care of some children. Her plan was to disguise herself as a nurse and to smuggle herself into the post. On the floor among the bodies there were quite a number of suitcases that those who were now dead had brought with them. Certainly she couldn't find a white coat, but she did find an old-fashioned nightgown with long sleeves which she put on and a white cloth which she tied around her head. On top of this she put a jacket, so that the old-fashioned style of the nightgown was not visible. Without saying a word, she slipped into the children's section of the medical post, where she picked up a child at once and began immediately to take care of it.

When the nurses noticed the intruder they were very frightened, but could not bring themselves to send her away. In the evening there was an order for all doctors and nurses to be "segregated." Because the patient had no papers, she could not go with them. She waited at the entrance of the SS office until the people returned who had not yet been sent to their death. When the little group passed her, she suddenly bent down as if to tie her shoe and in this way crept into the lines. She still didn't have the orange badge by which the survivors were identified and therefore had to hide in the medical post for several days before she was able to return to the ghetto.

Exactly how this happened was not clear in her story.

First she hid in the "Aryan" section, but some Poles recognized her and so she couldn't stay there. The only thing for her to do was to return to the ghetto.

There she went back to her workshop without anyone's discovering where she had been. Meanwhile, however, the situation had changed since the fire in the ghetto at Passover. It had become clear to the Jews that in a short while they would all be exterminated. So they decided to put a high price on their lives and smuggled in weapons, uniforms and food for which they had to pay incredible sums. There were bunkers and underground tunnels burrowed through the entire ghetto. Each bunker contained beds, radio, food and ammunition.

"Whatever happened, we wanted to die as patriots and not perish miserably as dogs!"

She described proudly how the young people, women as well as men, had taught themselves to handle arms and how they had acquired a real fighting spirit.

"You can't imagine what it meant, Jews in arms and uniforms. They weren't the enemy, they were friends—our people! And they were brave."

People became armed so heavily that one young Jew let himself be provoked to shoot a German on the street in broad daylight. The patient was present when it happened, and she described with unconcealed enthusiasm and triumph how the German fell and how the dirt splashed around him. "It felt good to see, but it wasn't very wise," was her comment. At four o'clock the next morning the Germans marched in with artillery, gas bombs and handgrenades.

The final destruction of the ghetto had begun.

At that point the patient began to tell what was surely the most difficult part of her experience: Some special instinct or intuition or "perhaps God," she said, smiling cynically, or at any rate some premonition seemed to have saved her from final destruction.

Ten minutes before the Germans marched in, her husband took her out of the house she was hiding in and put her in a bunker. That very house, she insisted, was the first to be destroyed by the troops.

Obviously it was difficult for her to put this part of her story into words. Intermittently she blushed and grew pale. "I'm getting quite sick from talking about it. I've only told it to two people besides you. I'm sure I'll go completely crazy."

She held her hands in front of her eyes and moaned: "My eyes! I have seen so much. My eyes hurt from all they've seen."

Although she was not pressed to continue and could just as well have stopped there, she went on, giving the impression that something within her was driving her to go on talking. She listened to her own words with a mixture of reluctance and terror.

For four months after the destruction of the Jewish section of Warsaw, she wandered from one bunker to another with a smaller and smaller group of people. They couldn't go anywhere in daylight, but for a while the surviving Jews could at least meet each other at night and exchange news of the day's happenings. During the day the Germans searched for the bunkers with tanks, bombs and poison gas, using Jewish prisoners as informers (giving them the hope that they might stay alive in this way).

In the first week the patient was hidden with 300 other people in a bunker meant for 60, without light, water or drainage, but with lice—thousands of them. No matter what they did, they couldn't get rid of them.

After a week the patient was saved, thanks to what she calls her "intuition." When she went out at night to get some water, she drank and washed herself. She had a feeling that she shouldn't go back to the bunker. Together with her husband and some friends, she stayed outdoors all night. When they returned in the morning, the shelter was empty. The same night the Germans had found it and had murdered all the Jews.

After searching for a while, the little group of survivors found a hiding place in another bunker, which at first seemed quite luxurious. There was water, an electric transformer, food and a radio. But it was deep in the ground and it was consequently very hot there. The people walked around half-naked, looking as white as chalk, moaning because they weren't getting enough air. They would press themselves around the ventilator through which fresh air arrived from above.

After a while they all got an irritating eczema. They sweated profusely, and their bodies were covered all over with red blisters.

One day the patient heard someone walking about over their heads, tapping, walking a little, and tapping again. She mentioned this to the others and thought that it might be an SS officer trying to find the hidden bunker by knocking. The others calmed her down, claiming it was all in her imagination. Several days in succession she heard these steps and the tapping. She tried to suppress her fear and believe that the others were right, that she had had acoustic imaginations.

The fifth day she didn't hear any more steps. Everything was quiet. But suddenly the lights went out, and gas bombs were thrown in at the bunker's entrance. The people started to moan, scream and run about wildly to avoid the gas that was seeping in. One could hear the Germans waiting outside the entrance; one could count on them not to enter the bunker for several hours, until the gas had thinned out.

There was a tunnel leading from that bunker to another bunker and on out into the open. Despite the panic, they succeeded in breaking down the door to the tunnel. But when the first five people had gone through, the tunnel collapsed. The remaining 17 panicked again, and it took some time before they calmed down sufficiently to dig their way through the part that had collapsed, despite the darkness and the gas.

When they finally reached the open, they had to hide in a cellar full of bodies, which the Germans wouldn't visit a second time. Everyone who had escaped from the bunker was terribly thirsty. The strongest got some water. The patient described her total obsession with the thought of water. She couldn't understand that she had to share it with the others. She wanted it all for herself and cried when she didn't get enough. Finally the water supply was so low that the people in the cellar started to drink their own urine.

For two weeks she was unable to take any solid foods. She was constantly coughing up green mucus. She lost her voice. She could only whisper. She also had palpitations and was short of breath. "And then the lice and the dying."

All around her were dead bodies, black and swollen, sometimes in pieces, and some half-burned bodies of children. There was a sweetish, thick, nauseating stench everywhere. "A person can't tell you the way it was, a person simply can't describe it all," she said. "Only tell me why I didn't die. I don't understand it. I'm so afraid."

Of the 22 people in the bunker, 17 died in the cellar. Among them was a girlhood friend of hers who screamed and gurgled all the time while the others tried by every means possible to stop her, in fear that the Germans would hear. For several days and nights she kept moaning, "I want to die, but I can't. What do you do to die? Why don't you help me?" In the end she was completely out of her wits and moving like a machine. "I'm going to the Germans. I want to get shot. I can't stand it any longer," she explained. It was impossible to keep her there. Her father, who was among the survivors, didn't want to let her go alone and so he followed her. They left the cellar in broad daylight. After a short while some shots were heard.

Later, at night, they found their bodies.

By the end of the second week after the gas attack only five survivors were left. The patient had not recovered to the extent that she dared leave the bunker at night and go to the secret meeting place in the ghetto.

There were only a very few Jews left. It seemed that no more bunkers remained for them to hide in. They couldn't do anything except live in the ruins of the burned-out houses.

These half-destroyed houses had no staircases, and therefore one had to climb up the walls. As they were speaking of this, dawn began to break. One of the survivors from the cellar had an anxiety attack. She was in her thirties and had a son of about ten. She threw herself down on the ground and screamed, "We have to die. We have to. We all have to die. Right now!"

Her son started to cry, and the others were afraid that the Germans would hear her. They could not quiet her desperate screaming and struggling. She wanted to go to the Germans to end the unbearable strain. She dragged her son with her; terror-stricken and weeping, he tried to resist. After a few steps she turned around and threw herself on the patient, biting and striking her and screaming, "You have to come, too. I insist. You have to die, too." The patient succeeded in freeing herself and running away. (She still has a scar on her knee from this attack.)

Nobody was able to restrain the screaming woman with her whimpering child. Shortly afterward, the Germans shot them.

At the break of dawn the patient, her husband and two other survivors climbed up to the fifth floor of a burned-out house and there they sat motionless from four in the morning to eleven in the evening. In the garden below the Germans were going about singing, whistling and urging their hounds to go hunting for people who were hiding.

"We had decided that, if a German climbed up, we would grab him by the neck and throw him down. It would have been wonderfully satisfying."

During the 17 hours she spent on the burned wall the patient developed a way of rocking the upper part of her body to keep from growing stiff, thus enabling her to stay in one spot.

The next day they spent hidden beneath a rubbish heap, where it was impossible to stay longer because of the stench and the rats.

The following night the patient had a dream which determined her future. She dreamed she was going up a staircase to freedom. At the top was standing an elderly lady whose features were those of a Polish woman she knew. The woman was beckoning and smiling, saying, "Come on up here to me, come up here to me!"

She woke up feeling relieved, and it was clear that she had to do everything possible to get out of the ghetto. (Later she found a secret hiding place with the woman of her dream.)

Several days afterward a gravedigger came to the ghetto and offered to take eight people through a secret tunnel that led to a cemetery. He wanted 2,000–3,000 zlotys per person for this.

The next day the patient and her husband decided to follow the gravedigger into freedom. By chance, however, they met a friend of theirs who invited them to come into the only bunker still remaining and of which they had not previously known.

Later it was discovered that six of the eight Jews who had followed the gravedigger were caught by the Germans.

But one day the patient had a sudden, indefinable sense of

anguish and left the bunker. She took the others with her, and they all moved into a cellar full of bodies. "The more corpses the better," she explained. In this cellar they were only several feet from the Germans patrolling the streets each day. They moved out, as they later learned, just in time. When she returned one night she saw that the Germans had completely destroyed the bunker.

Now there were no more than ten survivors left. It was obvious that they could no longer stay in the ghetto. At any cost they had to find a way out. By this time they had scarcely any food, and every night the patient dreamed of bread and potatoes. Even in the daytime she was haunted by the smell and taste of bread.

In the end the little group of the last survivors managed to discover an underground sewer that led from the ghetto to the free section. For days they struggled through water and mud. Suddenly they realized that the Germans must have heard them and were throwing handgrenades from the other end. "But," she said, "in the sewers we were kings. There we ruled." She laughed triumphantly and threw back her head.

By the time the little group had finally struggled through the sewer to the other end and had reached ground level, the patient was completely exhausted. Despite this, she succeeded in tidying herself up a bit so that no one would see that she had been living underground.

For many Jews their pallor—due to the long stay underground—proved to be fatal.

She colored her cheeks red with brickdust scratched from a wall and put on an elegant woolen coat which she had dragged about with her to wear when she reached freedom.

That was the seventh of August, 1943. She and her husband and a few companions were the only survivors.

She didn't see her husband after that. He joined the partisans immediately after the escape.

Here the patient interrupted her story, jumped up and shouted, "And now do you think I can have a child?" She started to mumble to herself, "I'm crazy. I'm stupid. I still can't sleep. And the child would be exactly the same." To my question of what the child would be like, she answered hesitantly and anxiously, "He would be mad, too. I want to go to Poland. I want to find my mother, more than anything else, my mother." And after a pause she added, "And, of course, my husband, too." When asked what she would do if she didn't find either of them, she answered without hesitation, "Then I'll put an end to it. Such a terrible life isn't worth living. I've seen too many dead. I'm so tired of all I've seen. If this [abortion] can't be arranged, then I'll put an end to myself, too. I have seen 50,000 people enter the gas chamber and for years I have lived among the dying and the dead. You won't understand me when I tell you this, but I have no fear of death." This last statement the patient made quite calmly, in a matter-of-fact way. It was a strange contrast to her earlier emotional, colorful and dramatic behavior. You got the feeling that this was not an empty threat.

She was granted a legal abortion, and in the fall of 1945 she went back to Poland. She has not been heard from since.

Postscript

The above account was submitted to the Swedish Board of Health in the summer of 1945. After it was published in *All Världens Berättare (All the Stories in the World)* in 1951, the magazine's editor, Carl Johan Rådström, said he had received many letters from readers doubting the authenticity of this document.

1967

Reaching Safety

W HEN WE TRY to survey the confused picture of psychopathological symptoms that appear in refugees shortly after they reach safety, we can observe the following characteristics:

At first—when the feeling of danger has passed—most refugees and former concentration-camp prisoners experience a short period of freedom and sometimes react in a slightly euphoric way. Later—after a few weeks or several months at the most—we can distinguish two groups of psychic disturbances. In one the reaction is primarily to the sudden social displacement; in the other the concern is less with the change of environment as such, but on the confrontation with a superior hostile power.

In both cases the abreaction to the traumatic experience may make social adjustment difficult or it may be considered an isolated symptom which doesn't impede the process of adaptation.

The first group shows a predominance of paranoid reactions which are often noisy and disturb the patient's environment, but in most cases they are harmless. Whether or not the refugee can overcome them depends—in my experience—not so much on his past, on his intelligence or on his social position, as on his age. Very young as well as elderly people have a tendency to remain paranoid, while middle-aged people seem to recover best.

The paranoid reaction is an attempt to reestablish contact with reality on a regressive magic basis.[1] The refugee, having suddenly and unexpectedly been forced to give up all social relationships with his home country, arrives helpless, without financial resources and without rights, in a new country. Quite often he is forced to accept help from others—individuals or institutions—and he must live on a lower social and economic level than he is accustomed to. Moreover, he is unfamiliar with both the way of life and the general mentality in the new country. It is difficult for him to make any contacts either in his private life or at work, and he has to start everything from the beginning. The feeling of being unwelcome is common among refugees; nobody can avoid it completely. The paranoid reaction is an effort to reverse this situation: the refugee moves from the fringes of society to its center. He is no longer an anonymous person—he is at the focal point of people's attention. His uncertainty and hostility are projected onto strangers he is dependent on. As the victim of their intrigues, he has the right to complain about them. This gives the refugee a considerable narcissistic satisfaction.

The following case shows a slightly paranoid reaction in a woman who otherwise behaved quite normally. It also shows how such reactions have a tendency to spread and must therefore be stopped as soon as possible.

A thirty-year-old woman who had been in Sweden for several months complained that she never got the right change back when she went shopping. Every time she went into a store, all the other customers were served before her. One day, she said, a saleswoman in a big department store had indignantly turned her back on her when she wanted to buy something. When she considered more closely the way in which she was conducting herself, she discovered herself that it had actually been her own behavior that provoked the treatment she had received. It was her habit to stand, uncertain and embarrassed, in the background and let other people go ahead of her. When she asked for what she wanted, her voice became so shaky and indistinct that the very busy saleslady couldn't be sure that she had said anything at all.

The patient felt that the general attitude toward refugees in Sweden was exactly the same as the one she felt she had experienced.

She was completely lacking in insight into her difficulties. She first visited me to discuss the problems her daughter was having at school, but it soon became obvious that the daughter had adopted a paranoid attitude from her mother. The child felt she was being badly treated both by other pupils and by the teachers. When the mother clearly understood her false evaluation of the situation, not only did her own paranoid attitude disappear, but the child's as well, without any treatment.

An important factor in the development of the paranoid reaction is ignorance. Even during the First World War it was observed that prisoners living among people whose language they didn't understand felt pursued and were convinced that people wanted to kill them.[2] Every day less drastic instances of misunderstanding arise out of the refugee's ignorance.

A young girl who had come to Norway as a refugee complained that the family she worked for several times a week didn't like her, and she felt they wanted to get rid of her. Had they been unkind to her? "Oh, no." After some hesitation she said: "I get nothing but fish for dinner; and that's because they don't want to cook real food on days when I'm in the house." The young girl didn't know that in Norway fish is common, everyday food, whereas in her own country it isn't regarded as "real" food. Somewhat stronger paranoid reactions occurred in a sixty-year-old natural scientist who had been highly respected in his homeland but who suddenly had been forced to flee—precipitately—to Sweden. On his arrival he asked a younger member of his family, who had already spent quite some time in Sweden, to help him find exactly the work that would make it possible for him to enjoy a position similar to the one he had had in his own country. As a matter of fact, he had some chance to get such a position. Yet several months of uncertainty and expectation passed by. The elderly man, who wasn't used to being without work, became restless and nervous and began to avoid people. He was afraid of permitting himself any enjoyment or entertainment. He rented a cheap room and ate little. He was obsessed with the thought that he was a burden to the refugee organization and that he was dependent on their economic aid. At the same time he became more and more impatient. He wasn't accustomed to asking for help.

Suddenly one day he paid a visit to his young relative and tried to strangle him. He was completely beside himself. Screaming, he claimed that the young man was working against him, saying that he was too old, conservative and old-fashioned to be considered for the opening in question. Because of his violent agitation, all efforts to prove that his reproaches were unfounded failed.

After some time he achieved a position in keeping with his qualifications. Once again he was a composed, balanced man. When a discussion touched on the described episode, he would try to minimize its importance and claim that the young man had always been an insolent rascal and it certainly wouldn't harm him if someone gave him a good spanking. This attitude, however, prevented him from becoming good friends once again with his young relative.

This episode demonstrates clearly that behind paranoid ideas there is a false evaluation of reality. The reasons the paranoid person gave in this case for his apparent defeat could very well have been true, because the young man had actually opposed him on the grounds of his conservatism. But this opposition hadn't prevented him from being loyal or from doing everything he could to help the older man.

It was apparent that the man's paranoid ideas were a form of self-criticism that he projected onto his environment. He himself had the feeling that he was too old for the intended position and that he hadn't kept up with the newer developments in his field as well as he should have. This would probably never have bothered him if he hadn't suddenly been forced to move from his familiar social environment, which meant that he lost a great deal of the social respect and security he had enjoyed in his native country.

Such paranoid reactions are typical not only of refugees, but also of immigrants in general, and as such have been mentioned by many writers. Next to psychotherapy the dissemination of abundant information about the refugee's new environment—cultural as well as material—is the best way of preventing such reactions. And of course the refugee must learn the new language; otherwise he will remain helplessly isolated.

Whereas the paranoid reaction is a characteristic commonly shared by refugees and immigrants, the second type of reaction, which is marked by a traumatic encounter with the enemy, has many things in common with the war neuroses found among soldiers.

Refugees who had been in special danger before and during their flight and those who had actively participated in underground work belong to the second group. All former concentration-camp prisoners—who over a long period of time were exposed to such an intense psychological and physical stress that someone who hasn't experienced it would hardly be able to imagine it—also belong to this group. The sense of abandonment and impotence in relation to lowered physical resistance makes the enemy's ruthlessness seem like an overwhelming unconscious command: you must cease to resist, you must despise yourself, you must die.

All those who have been in more or less direct contact with the pressure of the Nazis—either through propaganda, persecution, or resistance movements or in prisons—have had to struggle on two fronts at the same time, resist the outer enemy and fight the inner impulse to surrender.

Jean-Paul Sartre is one of the few people who have understood this tragic inner collaboration between the pursuer and the pursued:

> A moment comes when torturer and tortured are in accord, the former because he has in a single victim symbolically gratified his hate of all mankind, the latter because he can only bear his fault by pushing it to the limit, and because the only way he can endure his self-hatred is by hating all other men along with himself.[3]

The enemy's overwhelming cruelty, hatred and contempt may weaken the individual's sadomasochistic inhibitions. Sperling differentiates between people who feel an urge to submit and those who revolt against the enemy's command.

> Those who obey "the command to die" had only to transgress a little, to be killed by their torturers; or they exchanged the minimum food rations for cigarettes. Another interpretation of the traumata was the command to be reckless, selfish, cruel, and suspicious like the enemy, to throw off all decency, love, and confidence in human nature, trust in friends, etc.[4]

I am under the impression that we are not concerned with two clearly defined groups, but that the two motives could be found in one and the same person. The impulse to submit to the enemy and die appeared more or less clearly in all those who, in one way or another, had been exposed to the overwhelming pressure of the enemy. This is one of the causes for the well-known depression of refugees. The unconscious identification with the enemy seems to come later. It is a desperate attempt to ward off the individual's fear of passive surrender and the annihilation of one's own self.

The inner connection between these two alternatives is relatively apparent only in the following case, which also shows that not only soldiers and prisoners but also refugees who have had only indirect contact with the enemy experience this conflict.

A forty-year-old refugee who had been living in Sweden for some time sought psychoanalytic treatment because he suffered from insomnia and a fear of going insane. Both these symptoms had appeared after he came to Sweden. He seemed intelligent and well balanced. His friends valued his judgment because he was able to keep cool and not let himself be carried away by his emotions. He had had good vocational training in his native country and later obtained a job in another field of work. Ever since he was young, he had actively participated in politics. During the last few years before his escape, he had been living illegally in his native country and had played quite an important part in the resistance, in which he had shown great self-control and courage. He managed to escape to Sweden at the last moment, after he found out that his closest friends and collaborators had been arrested at a meeting which he himself should have attended but, by pure chance, didn't get to in time.

In Sweden he succeeded quite well in adjusting to the new conditions, although he could never quite accept the fact that he had to change professions. He was married, and the marriage seemed harmonious. His wife and child had accompanied him into exile.

I got the impression that he had always had some neurotic traits, a certain long-windedness, pedantry and difficulty in making quick decisions, but they were so well anchored in his personality that they did not seem to disturb his psychic balance.

During the treatment it became evident that his insomnia was due to a fear of falling asleep and having nightmares. He went to bed as late as possible in a state of total fatigue, hoping that this would prevent him from dreaming. His nightmares, which always contained acts of violence against people while he himself helplessly looked on, generally ended with a terrible fear that he would never wake up again. He himself understood that this represented his fear of death.

In connection with these nightmares he talked about a familiar theme for all refugees: the sense of guilt toward their comrades. He had saved his own skin while his friends had been captured and put into concentration camps. He knew very

well that his own imprisonment wouldn't have been of any use
to them or to the cause they were fighting for. But these rational arguments didn't help. He kept on brooding over this
idea, a frame of mind that was followed by attacks of anxiety
and gloom.

Would he have been able to resist the enemy? Would he
have been able to sustain his assurance and self-respect, or
would he have become a miserable character who hated himself, crouching before those who tortured him? At the same
time he was convinced that his comrades, one and all, had had
the strength to withstand torture and humiliation without betraying anything or debasing themselves. The more he glorified
them, the lower his self-esteem fell.

At that point his fear of going insane increased. He felt he
would suddenly go out of his mind and pounce upon another
human being in order to torture and kill him.

It was clear that his impulse to murder was a desperate escape from the fear of becoming a victim of the enemy. For him
there was only one way of escaping that fate: by adopting the
enemy's behavior and sadism and by killing like him.

But at the moment he realized that his impulse to murder
was a last, desperate revolt against his own weakness, he also
saw through the enemy. "The Nazis despise themselves and
cringe in front of their leader," he said, adding after a little
while, "They howl and march in troops because they're frightened and weak."

He had found a new way to resist his enemy, not by becoming like him but by seeing through him. This gave him both
emotional and moral satisfaction.

The insomnia and the fear of going insane proved to be real
neurotic symptoms that appeared in reaction to the reduced
inhibitions of his sadomasochistic impulses. His traumatic experience of enemy atrocities (committed not only upon himself
but also upon his comrades) had caused this weakening of
inhibitions.

This patient's problems were probably typical symptoms of

the great majority of refugees who had been in enemy hands or had come close to it. The conflict is kept unconscious by means of a wide range of neurotic symptoms. However, occasionally we may find that people who have spent a long time in concentration camps have adopted some of the enemy's ideas and behavior without realizing it themselves.

In the summer of 1945 some young women employees of a company in Stockholm went on strike because their employers wanted to shorten their lunch hour on Saturday. There were also some foreign girls, former concentration-camp prisoners, working in the company. They were shocked by the demands of the Swedish girls and declared that they ought to have been in *Buchenwald!* Finally, the Swedish girls were fired. In a newspaper interview the foreign girls said that they were "delighted by the dismissal."

Self-contempt and an unconscious identification with the enemy may become an integral part of the personality. This seems to be one of the main causes of the asocial behavior that concentration-camp prisoners and displaced persons so often display (such as anti-anti-Semitic attitude in people who consciously disclaim all race discrimination).

"Life in a concentration camp doesn't produce democrats," a former concentration-camp prisoner assured me. He knew what he was talking about, although he himself had been able to preserve his faith in democracy and human dignity. Well-developed ego ideals and an active, positive attitude toward the country and the people you are imprisoned for seem to be the only counterbalance that can prevent a moral, emotional and physical breakdown. The awareness that you are not imprisoned because you have broken the law for your own profit but that you are suffering misery and humiliation for a common cause seems to be a life-sustaining factor of unsuspected importance. The apparently meaningless becomes significant and an inner bond with the world outside the concentration camp is maintained. Mortality among Danish criminal prisoners in German concentration camps was 30 percent, whereas the mortality among Danish political prisoners was 13 percent.

However, I have the impression that manifestations of asocial behavior have not been the most obvious trait among displaced persons.

Most of those who have written about the subject have noted the prisoners' "emotional apathy" or "shallowness of feelings." It is expressed not only as a lack of interest in the fate of other people but also as a terrifying indifference to one's own self.

During the Second World War refugees who visited the outpatient clinics in the hospitals of Stockholm had a higher rate of absenteeism in the latter part of their treatment than the local inhabitants. Those suffering from tuberculosis had a tendency to neglect their checkups afterward. When the nurse called on them personally to remind them about it, they promised to go but "forgot" it.

Patients who had an appointment for a certain day and hour would either get there a day early or a day late; or else at the wrong hour on the appointed day. Today, tomorrow and next week were vague concepts for them. It seems as though many of them had stopped thinking of and planning for the future.

Emotional apathy and shallowness, or the feeling that you are "an empty skin," describe the state of mind that afflicts prisoners in the camps and that persists afterward for some time. Under favorable social conditions it disappears without treatment.

In psychotherapy these patients are often remarkably passive and uncommunicative. However, in contrast to other neuroses, their silence is hardly a sign of unconscious resistance. It is the silence of the cemetery. Large portions of the personality seem to have died. Much can be revived, but many will always have white spots that are just like the white spots on the map of a bombed ciy, bearing witness to the fact that life once pulsated there.

Chronic malnutrition, dirt, and vermin, disease and ill-treatment, combined with a daily experience of destruction and death, seemed to make the prisoners feel completely powerless. The authentic verification of reality was replaced by magic, animistic thinking; object relationships were weakened; sexual needs disappeared, and the prisoners regressed to the primitive oral stage.

The following case may illustrate how thoroughly a personality may disintegrate. The young man concerned had, despite everything, enough of a will to survive to be able to undergo brief psychoanalytic treatment. No doubt a complete account of his story will describe the process of recovery such people go through better than any theoretical discussion would.

The patient was a young man, about twenty-five years old, of Polish-Jewish extraction. Despite his slow reactions, his vague, long-winded answers and the laconic way in which he occasionally expressed himself, he seemed intelligent. He spoke fluent Polish, German and Hebrew. Later it became evident that he had a good sense of humor, something you didn't notice at first.

The patient had been several years in Auschwitz and half a year in Belsen. He came to Sweden as a refugee and didn't want to return to Poland. He stayed first at a camp in southern Sweden and later at a smaller camp near Stockholm. On his arrival in Stockholm he was given clothes, money and lodgings by the Jewish community—as well as a wristwatch, which he displayed, radiant with joy. He had learned a trade and he had good chances of getting work.

But then difficulties arose. He had begun to worry, to feel abandoned, to sleep badly, when he came for analytic treatment. It soon became apparent that he was afraid of standing on his own two feet, of supporting himself and taking a job. He thought it was impossible to stand for eight hours in a shop and work hard. He complained like a small child and tried to get the analyst to protect him. Unconsciously he was hoping that the analysis would deliver him from working and that it would help him get public assistance. He did get it for a couple more months, but then he was feeling so good that he started

looking for a job, on his own initiative. He managed to perse-
vere despite sporadic impulses to give up.

His passivity and wish to be taken care of, as well as his
fear of responsibility, had their roots in his childhood, but they
had become fixed and pathologically reinforced during the
many years he spent in the concentration camps.

The patient and his younger sister had grown up in a small
Polish village with a relatively large Jewish community. His
deeply religious father was something of a patriarch and had
broad philosophical interests. When he wasn't working in his
workshop, he would sit in his study reading. He tried to be just
and strict with the children, but he was so tenderhearted that he
often gave in to them. The mother, who was less religious, took
good care of the household. When the children had to be com-
forted or rewarded, this was always done by giving them extra
portions of good food.

The parents looked down on Poles, because they thought
they were far below their own cultural level, and they admired everything German. "You can say what you like," he
told me one day, "but before Hitler came to power Germany
was a civilized nation."

The family centered around the children. The parents, who
seem to have had a happy marriage, had only one wish: that
the children be protected from a harsh and hostile environment as long as possible. Until the boy had reached the age of
about ten or twelve, his mother accompanied him to school
in order to protect him from the other boys who used to throw
stones at the Jewish children.

The father, who worked hard himself to provide for the
family, let the boy go to school as long as possible. When at
last the son had finished school and started working in his
workshop, he got only small jobs. "Father didn't want children
or adolescents to work," said the patient. "We were supposed
to enjoy ourselves."

The idyllic family life ended abruptly when the Germans
invaded Poland. The whole family was sent to Auschwitz.

There he lost contact with his mother and sister. After several months he was told that they were dead. He lived with his father and witnessed his death, which may well be regarded as suicide. The old man refused to eat food that wasn't compatible with Jewish ritual. After a short while he literally starved to death. The father's example asserted a strong moral pressure upon him. But he didn't give up. He ate everything he could get hold of.

Life in the camp was the same for him as for everybody else. They starved; they toiled; they got very little sleep. They were mistreated, and they saw others being mistreated.

In the beginning of the analysis the patient was preoccupied with telling how the Germans had tormented his fellow prisoners. He got excited, talked very fast and sometimes interrupted himself with a short, scornful laugh. It was obvious that his scorn was aimed not at the oppressor but at the oppressed. For a long time that was the only sign of spontaneous emotional reaction. He talked about his own experiences in the camps in the manner of objective, matter-of-fact reporting, without personal commentary, as if he were talking about another person.

Often he returned to two episodes that he described over and over again and each time they revealed the extreme forms that human passivity and lack of will power may take.

Within a period of a few weeks he was sent to the gas chambers three times. SS officers had picked him out and forced him to undress. Then he was given an overcoat and sent barefoot—this was in the middle of winter—to the gas chamber together with a group of other people who had been sentenced to death in the same fashion. Each time, at the last moment, an SS officer came cycling after him, picked him out and took him back to the camp. This SS officer treated the patient like some kind of lapdog which had to obey when he whistled but which he, in turn, protected from the other guards.

The other episode took place in Belsen two days before the prisoners were rescued by the allied troops. The patient was so weak that his fellow prisoners thought he was dead. They put him on the pile of corpses. While he was lying there, he thought, "Since I'm lying here among the corpses, I must be dead," and was unable to move. After he had been lying there for one day and two nights, the English came and cleared away the pile. A soldier grabbed him and shouted, "But he's alive!" The patient thought, "If he says I'm alive, then I'm not dead."

He left the decision of his own life and death to the discretion of other people.

When the patient wasn't talking about his past experiences but was considering his present situation, the thing that seemed to occupy all his thoughts was food.

He began one of the very first sessions by asking, "Where's the black market?" I told him it didn't exist, because rations were plentiful. He retorted in some excitement, "But don't you see, I've got to have more butter!" After a few days he appeared again, very pleased and smiling, asking, "Would you like some butter?" "Where did you get it?" "On the black market, of course," he answered triumphantly.

Not only did the patient have a big dinner and breakfast every day, but he also consumed an astounding amount of sweets, chocolate and pastry. When he had something that tasted sweet in his mouth, the world around him would disappear. He could stand for hours in front of the central railway station in Stockholm, munching candy and waiting. "What do you wait for?" I asked him. "I don't know," he said. "Perhaps I am waiting for some of my old friends. Maybe some of them will come to Stockholm." Needless to say, he always waited in vain. When he stood there as in a trance, waiting and waiting, he was waiting not for the living but for the dead. It was as if he hadn't quite yet realized that they were dead.

His excessive desire for food also had obvious destructive tendencies. Without planning it, he consumed enormous quantities, and in that way grew fat and swollen. He began to sweat profusely and to suffer from chronic constipation. He had blood in his feces and had to get medical treatment.

This reckless eating ended when the patient had a severe attack of anxiety while having breakfast at a restaurant. He was pale when he came to the session; he groaned, sweated and rolled restlessly on the couch. "I've seen the evil eye, and I've been sick and completely out of my mind the whole day."

He displayed a strong aversion to saying anything more about the incident, but he felt so sick and anxiety-ridden that he saw no other way out than thinking the matter over and trying to understand what had happened.

"I was sitting in a restaurant eating sandwiches. And there was a man who kept looking at me. He had the evil eye. And then I had to go to the bathroom and vomit. That's all."[5]

It was obvious that the patient believed it was possible for people to have the evil eye. I asked him what kind of sandwich he had eaten. "A ham sandwich," he added in an angry, defiant tone. He was silent for a long time; then he said quietly, but with a certain agitation in his voice, "If Father had seen that, he'd have beaten me to death."

Was it actually possible that his kind, gentle father that he had known in reality had been transformed in his imagination into a sadistic creature who threatened his life when he didn't observe the religious precepts?

It seemed that the image of the father had merged with that of the enemy (perhaps this was facilitated by the father's admiration of everything German). Inasmuch as the father chose to starve to death rather than break the religious precepts, the son felt this was an unconscious command. "Do as I do. You must not eat." That is to say: you shall not live; you shall die.

The Nazi slogan against the Jews had the same content: "*Juda verrecke!*" means "*Juda* [the Jewish people], starve to death!"

The patient managed to resist both the father's and the enemy's demands. He survived. But the self-destructive tendency of his eating showed that it was a compromise between revolt and submission. By eating excessively he was harming and destroying himself.

When he had worked through his fear of capitulating to the enemy and his feeling of guilt toward his father, his desire for food gradually decreased, and his constipation disappeared.

Shortly afterward he ended his analysis. He had fallen in love with a young girl and wanted to get married. "Now I want to save for the wedding, and I don't have any more time for analysis," he explained.

A year later he and his young wife emigrated to the United States. The patient had largely overcome his passive, dependent attitude. He was able to save money instead of spending it on sweets. For the first time in his life he was in love. He didn't live only for the present moment; he could plan for the future. He could look forward to a time that might bring him happiness.

Despite their goodwill, ordinary people often show a certain reticence and shyness toward refugees and former concentration-camp prisoners, i.e., toward the victims of Fascism. They are afraid of approaching them. These people are taboo. This attitude can be characterized as "a flight from one's self."[6] The existence of these men and women in our very midst reminds us that our evil dreams, which disappear with daybreak and which we thought belonged to the realm of shadows, may become a living reality.

2. YOUTH

Some remain on probation all their life—they are the eternal adolescents through whom the race matures.

—Arthur Koestler

The Young Man Luther and Present-Day Man

<hr>

ERIK ERIKSON'S study of Luther as a young man has a remarkable revelance for us today. It is an impassioned contribution by an author who is sensitive to the fluctuations in history and the individual's effort to find a meaningful place in an insecure, changing world. The man who wrote this book is deeply troubled. He sees the old ideals being threatened and cannot yet see new ones sprouting up around him. It is a cry of warning from a person who, through his work in therapy, knows how dangerous such a vacuum is, for a man without any convictions is at the mercy of the destructive forces both within and outside himself. This unease of the heart drives the author to discuss, within the framework of the book, Hitler and Chinese brainwashing as well as George Bernard Shaw. He does it brilliantly—though at times the unity of the book nearly gives way.

Luther's development and struggle, says Erikson, must be viewed as the experience of a sensitive person straddling two eras. In Luther, who lived during the transitional period between the late middle ages and modern times, this experience led to a religious crisis. He arrived at a new formulation of the relationship between God and man which expressed the general need, prevailing throughout his age, for a new orientation.

When we view Luther in a larger historical context and apprehend the universal human aspects of his problem, he appears once more as the person he was—and still is: a living force behind the struggle for freedom of the individual, a force that continues to influence modern man far beyond denominational lines. Luther arrived at a new equilibrium between external independence and internal responsibility, a new delineation between man's internal and external world. He has created a new consciousness of our own existence, verified by an uncompromising voice within man himself: it is the inner dialogue that gives us our identity.

Such a man arrived at a new sense of the individual's life by means of intensive struggle and suffering, and cannot be dismissed—as the psychiatrist Reiter contends—as a clear case of endogenous melancholia, lacking in *"innere Ausgeglichenheit"* (inner balance or repose, a simple enjoyment of life).[1] Nor is he a mere nihilist and *"Umsturzmensch"* (the kind of man who, without a plan of his own, wants to turn the world upside down),[2] as the Catholic priest Denifle would make him out to be. And one underestimates his despair and ruthless self-scrutiny if, like the Prussian professor of theology, you believe that Luther's whole message was *"vom höchsten Kriegsherren von oben befohlen"* ("even the highest military men take orders from above"). Erikson also polemicizes against a concept not uncommon in psychoanalysis according to which a human being is nothing but "the sum of his parents' mistakes." Knowledge of the significance of childhood conflicts in the life and personality of the adult is the prerequisite for helping a person to a new ethical orientation. Man has the possibility of using early experiences in different ways. He may sublimate them to serve universal human ideals. But on the basis of the same experience, he may also turn away from or even abuse them.

Erikson points out that no time of life affords an opportunity for spontaneous reorientation greater than that provided by adolescence. "The resources of tradition blend together with new resources within man, and in this way something absolutely

new is created, a new individual, and with this new individual
a new generation and with this a new era."

During this period of preparation—Erikson calls it a mora-
torium—Martin Luther experienced his childhood conflicts on
two levels, partly as extremely personal difficulties, partly as a
general conflict of his times. The twofold level explains the
frightening intensity of his struggle. He was among those people
"whose fate it is to experience all human problems heightened
to personal torment, to the agonies of hell." Like Erikson,
Hermann Hesse believes that "human life becomes true suffering, a hell, only during those times when two epochs, two cultures and religions intrude on each other."[3]

Erikson believes that a person achieves greatness not because
he has had a particular kind of conflict in his childhood, but by
virtue of the fact that he has managed to solve conflicts in a
universally applicable way which can become an example to
people of his generation.

Luther's childhood conflicts do not seem to have been especially uncommon. His father, who was of peasant stock, belonged
to a social group that was poised between two alternatives,
either a proletarization, which was worse than the living conditions he came from, or economic prosperity, social status and
power in the evolving bourgeoisie. Hans Luther achieved the
latter—at what expense to himself we know not—and left a
considerable fortune. Erikson believes that the father's harsh
treatment of his oldest son stemmed from his social ambitions.
The son was to achieve even more than the father. Here we see
how the social changes of the period affected the most intimate
relationship between father and son.

A much-quoted statement by Luther provides a key to understanding the emotional relationship between them. Luther mentions that his father hit him so hard that *"ich ihn flohe und
ward ihm gram bis er mich wieder zu sich gewöhnte"* ("I fled
him and I became sadly resentful toward him, until he gradually got me accustomed to him again").[4] This indicates that
even though Martin was mortally afraid of his father, he none-

theless could not hate him. Why not? Because Hans, his father, who would not allow his son to come close to him, was very attached to him nevertheless and in need of his love. And how can a son hate his unjust, cruel father when he knows that at the same time, deep down, his father yearns for his affection? The son's hate backfires on him. His sadness grows and, increasingly, he comes to blame himself. Martin's reaction to his father's intensive love/hate relationship to him was that he became more preoccupied "with matters of individual conscience, a preoccupation which went far beyond the requirements of religion as then practiced and formulated."[5] Perhaps he also discovered that externally he could please his father and yet at the same time, deep within him, feel the faint echo of an overwhelming hatred.

For a while, then, it seemed as if Martin would be a model son. He fulfilled all his father's expectations. He did extremely well on his examinations, and when he became Magister Artium, his father wrote to him respectfully in the third person *"Ihr"* form of "you." Martin's sudden conversion at the age of twenty shattered all his father's proud dreams for the future. On his way to Erfurt he realized that a thunderstorm was approaching. A bolt of lightning struck him to the ground, and he was seized by mortal anguish. All of a sudden he heard himself cry out to Saint Anne—his father's patron saint—that he wanted to become a monk. He kept his vow—against his father's will and despite the fact that soon after his conversion he regretted his promise. The successful son of a successful father abandoned his identity and disappeared behind the walls of a monastery merging with a mass of anonymous novices.

Luther's introspective disposition, his ability to distinguish clearly between the subjective experiences of the inner world and the objective facts of the outer world, is expressed in his sober description of this experience: "He never claimed to have seen or heard anything supernatural. He only records that *something in him* made him pronounce a vow before the *rest of him* knew what he was saying."[6]

His conversion can also be seen as the first step in becoming free from his father. Like St. Paul, he realized that there was an allegiance higher than that to worldly laws, represented by his father. And there could be no postponement of his new obligation to obey.

In the monastery he would serve another father, one whom he had himself chosen. This one, his spiritual father, would lead him to eternal life, whereas his natural father was relegated to "a merely physical and legal status."[7]

By rebelling against his corporeal father and replacing him with an invisible, universal God, without any demigods whatsoever in the form of saints, Luther represented, in modern times, "a progress in spirituality"[8] similar to the one Freud attributed to the influence Moses exerted on the Jewish people. His rebellion against his earthly father later turned into a struggle against what Nietzsche calls "the great and glorious force of evil that was strong enough to call upon itself the wrath of his lacerated soul." This evil force was the Roman papacy. That which he had not dared say to his father, or even to his teacher, he would hurl in rage at his worldly father in Rome.

When he was older, says Erikson, Luther could no longer maintain the uncompromising standards of his youth. Moses' commandment "Honor thy father" would also apply to princes. No doubt he himself scarcely noticed that God's countenance was about to change. It was becoming more and more like that of the "nobility." The older Martin Luther became, the more he came to resemble his earthly father. He was quick to hate, found it difficult to forgive and would tolerate neither disobedience nor dissent.

This life cycle also follows a course of development common to people everywhere. The fearlessness, the lofty ideas and unyielding attitudes of youth give way to the aging person's doubts and resignation. People have a tendency to slip back to the ideals and identifications of their early childhood that they've struggled so hard to overcome. The fact that the young man Luther's life crisis was able to take on such dramatic dimensions was due to a specific historical situation. In his acts he accomplished what many young men—before and after him—have dreamed of: challenging a whole world single-handed on the strength of nothing other than a personal conviction.

The time he spent in the monastery was a period of increased insights into his inner conflicts. He learned to delineate clearly between constructive and destructive forces, between that which he thought came from God and that which came from the devil.

Luther entered the monastery because he wanted to talk with God, directly and without guilt feelings. But he didn't dare to. God's countenance would reveal such an overpowering wrath that it would destroy him. But the longing for the out-stretched hand of the forgiving father went on burning within him. His description of Jesus in Gethsemane bears the stamp of personal experience: "He [Christ] still loved the Father utterly, but the pangs, exceeding his strength, drove his innocent and weak nature to groan, cry, shudder and flee, just as without sin he sank beneath the weight of the cross."[9]

Luther himself said that he was not troubled by a desire either for gold or for women, but he trembled at the thought of the menacing voice inside him that was familiar with his deep, hidden hatred for his father and God.

No matter what he did, no matter how much he confessed, he discovered with his unerring psychological insight that "the deepest sins cannot be confessed because they are not even recognized, just as David, after committing murder and adultery, was not contrite until convicted by the rebuke of the prophet,"[10] as Bainton so clearly and simply puts it.

The man who saved him from these speculations was his father confessor Staupitz. For Luther, he became the good father who gave him what his real father had not been able to offer: warmth, kindness and humor combined with common sense and a surprising degree of psychological insight.

When Luther had confessed for six hours straight (did he suspect that this self-torment also included a quality of aggressiveness directed at the patient listener?), Staupitz interrupted him with a half-joking exclamation: "If you are going to confess so much, why don't you go out and do something worth confessing, such as killing your father or your mother instead of trotting in with these dollie's sins?"[11] What psychotherapist today would dare to give similar "counseling" when confronted by the endless self-complaints of a melancholic individual?

Luther's friendship with this fatherly teacher may have provided him the possibility of fusing the wise and understanding face of the Augustinian monk with that of his father, which he remembered as being distorted by hatred and anger. In his lecture on the Epistles to the Romans, he describes this development: "Whereas before the 'Justice of God' had filled me with hate, now it came to be inexpressibly sweet in greater love."[12] We can recognize the great liberation from anxiety and hatred (his own or his father's?) in the often quoted words: "He who sees God as angry does not see Him rightly but looks upon a curtain, as if a dark cloud had been drawn across His face."[13]

His ambivalence still remained, but he had accepted it and transferred it to a higher level:

> Observe now that when God was far He was at the same time near. He was far because Christ had used the word "forsaken," He was near because Christ said, "*My* God."[14]

The father's ambivalence, he realizes, is also the son's. God's anger is also an expression of his compassion. With this perception, Erikson says, it was possible for Luther to forgive God for being a father and do him justice. God—like his earthly father—was in need of the devotion of human beings. Luther's newly acquired trust in the father is expressed clearly in Stählin's words: "Man's road to God leads not to the goal. To acknowledge God's way to man, according to Luther, implies faith. Faith is to be like a child once more."[15]

Luther's first lectures at the University of Wittenberg were, in Erikson's opinion, a cathartic process that freed him from being plagued by obsessions. Luther discovered that man can achieve inner freedom and greater outer mobility by consistently using an introspective method with the religious writing as a medium.[16]

One might ask whether Luther would have been able to change his concept of God without an unconscious identification with Dr. Staupitz. A person who feels he is thoroughly hated and rejected is not able to rebel. He is able to stand alone only if he knows that there is someone who loves him, despite everything. It is possible that Luther felt that his confessor sanctioned his critical attitude. Staupitz himself seems to have been an unprejudiced man and also a reformer within the Augustine order. And had not Staupitz invited him to Wittenberg and later transferred to him the chair he himself had occupied?

Luther's categorical repudiation of the concept of free will is in keeping with his idea of the two faces of God. God's hatred of mankind was "a hatred not only on account of demerits and the works of free will, but a hatred that existed even before the world was created,"[17] Huizinga remarks in regard to Luther's concept of God. But even here, despite the pessimism, we can discern the son's indulgent attitude toward the father. He came to understand that his father had always been like that, long before he himself had come into the world. The son realizes that he is not an instigator, but is content to be a small spark that sometimes ignites a barrel of gunpowder.

Luther's newly acquired belief in God the Father was accompanied by a change in his balance of activity and passivity. He no longer needs to waste his energy on incessant complaints, against either God or himself. When, by means of his sermons in Wittenberg, Luther overcame his anguish at God's wrathful countenance, he was able to admit to his need for passivity. He could accept it because now there was once more someone who gave, without counting either his sins or his merits. And Luther, on the other hand, stopped interfering with the affairs of God the Father and of nature just as a mature person abandons his efforts to change his parents.

Der Sommer ist hart vor der Tür
Der Winter ist vergangen
Die zarten Blumen gehen herfür
Der das hat angefangen
Der wird es auch vollenden.

("The winter is gone/ And summer is at the door/ The flowers are coming up/ Whoever had begun such a process/ Will surely complete it.")[18]

One wonders whether Luther would have been able to develop this confident repose in the universe had he not encountered so much human kindness in the face of one individual—in that of Dr. Staupitz. By this means his latent energy was freed. During the several years that followed he became one of the leading warriors of the Renaissance.

Luther the man and his contributions are especially fascinating to us today because, as Stählin says, "he anticipates crucial discoveries in modern depth psychology." His work has developed with time into a moral strength in modern man's secular feeling of responsibilty for himself and others.

Luther understood that the Word itself was the connecting link in the inner dialogue between the self and its conscience. St. Augustine's statement that man had to hear before he could see is transformed by Luther in the spirit of the Renaissance. We acquire our identity by using the inner instrument God has given us: I am because I perceive the voice inside me.

Four hundred years later psychoanalysis would confirm this power of the word by demonstrating that the conscience consists primarily of acoustical impressions, of commands and restrictions the child has heard its parents say. In the same way that the Word and the inner dialogue led Luther to a deepened insight about himself, the word—the secular word—became the healing medium of psychoanalytic treatment. Language creates an internal unity in a person and new ties with his outer world.

In Luther's notes from his lectures on the Epistles to the

Romans, there is a sentence that could well be a statement of principle for all modern psychotherapy: "Perfect self-insight is perfect humility; perfect humility is perfect knowledge; perfect knowledge is perfect spirituality."[19] By emphasizing the psychological and social significance of the word, Luther, like Erasmus, created an entirely new medium of human expression. To a certain degree this occurred at the cost of the visual arts. It is no mere coincidence that music, the most abstract of art forms, flourished during that period. The music of Bach—next to Luther's chorale *"Eine feste Burg ist unser Gott"* ("A Mighty Fortress Is Our God")—is the highest artistic expression of Protestantism.

But the word leads to criticism—inasmuch as no position is taken so long as it is not expressed in words—as well as to the rejection of external ceremony. Erasmus simply considered the Mass of his time a spectacle of human stupidity. The instrument of language, over which both had such a great command (even though each in his own manner), led them back to the origins, to textual interpretation and Bible criticism.

Luther's translation of the Bible into German—a German which in its rich and colorful realism can be compared only to Shakespeare's English—had a profound psychological effect, which the translation of the Bible by Erasmus from Greek to Latin couldn't have. Luther's language evidently had an overwhelming influence on his contemporaries. Albrecht Dürer, one of the leading artists of the age, breaks out of his own visual mode of expression to favor the word. When he painted his last big painting, *The Four Apostles,* he added texts to it that he had selected himself from Luther's translation of the New Testament, published in September 1522.

With Luther, the conscience began speaking the mother tongue. Pascal may have had a similar significance in the French language. It became more difficult to defend oneself against the judgment of conscience when orders and restrictions were no longer given in an abstract foreign language without points of reference in everyday life. Here, too, we can see a parallel with psychoanalytic treatment. It is considered much more effective if the patient speaks in his own language, the language that first struck his ear and which with time developed into the voice within him.

This new consciousness of language led to the recognition of the significance of psychic motivations in human actions. Man could no longer be satisfied with impersonal mechanical absolution. He is no longer able to get rid of either authentic gold or justified self-criticism. Luther, Erikson says, "rejected all arrangements whereby a collection of saints made it unnecessary for man to grasp the full extent of his life's suffering." He had the courage to accept his sense of being damned, a feeling he had earlier tried to fight. He exhibits a deep psychological understanding when he says: "They are damned who flee damnation."[20] Today we know that man's unconscious efforts to defend himself against guilt feelings only chain him even more tightly to his superego, which already is too severe.

Upon scrutiny, the infantile notion that one presented Our Lord with a list of good deeds and with that awaited his reward, or, as Stählin says, "We serve God so that God will perform services for us," becomes untenable. Luther understood that the mortification of the flesh and sexual abstention do not liberate us from the suspicion that our acts have been motivated by indifference, egotism or hatred rather than by "faith, love, desire and will." This attitude led to his conception that men and women should live together as an essential part of our human existence. Luther regarded celibacy as a kind of suicide. Yet he maintained that a life of chastity was, after all, worth striving for.

According to Luther's interpretation, the individual stood alone before his God without being able to refer to mitigating circumstances. He was forced to "live alone, die alone, and be saved alone," as Bainton says, and—one is tempted to add—to take sole responsibility for himself.

Here Luther anticipates modern man's loneliness and tragic sense of life. Suffering, sorrow and guilt are inevitable in a person's life. The paradisiacal dream of happiness, of everlasting sunshine, is a picture out of a child's storybook and has no equivalent in the reality we live in. The question in Luther's twenty-ninth thesis—"Who knows whether all souls in purgatory wish to be redeemed . . . ?"—expects no reply. It is a fanfare and a challenge.

Those involved in psychoanalytic research—at times somewhat against their own will—have also acknowledged that human development is inconceivable without deep inner conflicts. One of our time's most eminent psychiatrists and psychoanalysts, Franz Alexander, introduces his study on the total personality with Goethe's words: *"Drum willst Du Dich von Leid bewahren, so flehe zu den Unsichtbaren, dass sie zum Gluck den Schmerz verleihen."* (Therefore if you want to save yourself from sorrow, implore the omniscient forces, perhaps by good fortune they'll take on your pain.)

Luther understood that "conscience is the inner foundation on which we and God have to learn to live with each other as husband and wife." But he also knew that we can sometimes be happy—very happy, in fact. A psychoanalyst would say that the ego and the superego can exist peacefully side by side. Occasionally tensions will arise between them, but if they are overcome in a positive manner, this may lead to new sublimations, to greater maturity.

Luther's rock-hard determinism may have resulted not alone from his resignation to his father's unpredictable emotional fluctuations. With his talent for introspection, which was focused on the psychological motivations for our actions, he may have known all too well that man's experience of free will arises under the pressure of harsh reality. It has inexorably forced us to curtail our own impulses. Thus freedom of the will ultimately becomes the sense of satisfaction we get when we have met the demands our conscience has imposed upon us.

Luther considers human will to resemble "a riding beast [that] stands in the middle between God and the devil and which is mounted by one or the other without being able to move toward either of the two contending riders"[21] (quoted according to Huizinga). This deeply pessimistic outlook is in some respects fairly close to modern depth psychology. Freud,

who entered psychology by way of his studies in the natural
sciences, says in his autobiography that he adheres adamantly
to a psychic determinism "as to a prejudice." His description
of the plight of the ego "urged on by the id, attacked severely
by the superego, repulsed by reality," ends with the outburst:
"Indeed, it is not easy to be alive."

Only during the past ten years have those involved in psychoanalytic research begun to protest against Freud's pessimism. More and more often it is claimed that, despite the
ways in which the ego is confined, it nevertheless has a certain
independence. It is able to develop its own activity, something
Freud doubted.

But the resemblance between a determinism that is carried
out consistently and an insistence on man's inability to break
out of a causal context, the tragic imperfection of human existence, should not conceal the basic difference between Luther's
attitude and Freud's.

In Luther's opinion man was evil and corrupt from the time
of his birth. He could not on his own strength do anything for
his salvation but was forced to wait passively for God to care
about him. The father's need for a child is more important than
the child's need for a father. Freud, the natural scientist, was
aware of nature's healing forces, which exist in each person. The
task of the psychotherapist is limited to the removal of harmful
obstacles: nature does the rest. Freud admits that he does not
understand the stages of the therapeutic process. He quotes an
old French proverb: "I bandage him and God cures him!" He
had a fundamental trust in nature's own healing power that
Luther lacked. But then, too, Freud was the oldest son of a
mother whose love he never had any cause to doubt. The same
cannot be said of Luther. Erikson doesn't go into his relationship
with his mother at any length. But you get the feeling that behind his discussion with father and God, with the inner voice,
there is an even deeper despair without words: the desolation a
person feels when he has not experienced that first maternal love
and warmth.

Freud sometimes exhibits a belief in the triumph of nature,

of reason and of moderation that brings him closer to Erasmus. Also his education was well rooted in the ancient culture. He was what Erasmus so much wanted to be: a cosmopolitan. In his pamphlet *Why War* he writes: "The ideal condition of things would of course be a community of men who had subordinated their instinctual life to the dictatorship of reason." But, sad and resigned, he adds later: "An unpleasant picture comes to one's mind of mills that grind so slowly that people may starve before they get their flour."[22]

In a time when democratic people are exposed to the enticements of authoritarian ideologies and are personally burdened by questions of their own function and right to exist within the borders of their own society, a rediscovery of the deed of the young Luther is a welcome reorientation and a renewed awareness of the European's historical origin. Erikson again conjures up the image of the young man in Worms who stood alone against Emperor and Church, against banishment and the threat of death. He spoke up not for an established faith. He referred neither to his ancestors nor to tradition. He spoke from his own personal conviction, in order to preserve his own inner identity. That was all—and that was a great deal.

> If then your majesty and the princes want a very simple answer, I will give it without much ado. Unless I am convicted by Scripture and plain reason—I do not accept the authority of the popes and councils. . . . I cannot and I will not recant anything, for to go against conscience is neither right nor safe."[23]

"Here I take my stand, I can do no otherwise." Certainly, he did not say that, but the image of the legend does not lack a striking psychological relevance.

When Abraham refrained from sacrificing Isaac, he acted, Dewey believes, in accord with his own inner voice, which dissociated itself from the human sacrifice. In this way he gave the human conscience a new dimension: consideration and care for the life of another human being. It seems to me that Luther assumes the same kind of attitude in the development of this, as Freud puts it, "phylogenetically earliest instance in our psychic personality," by pointing out man's obligation to act in agreement with his own inner norms—even if this may cause him conflict with the world around him.

Luther, who in accordance with the philosophy of the middle ages believed that earthly serfdom and spiritual freedom were not mutually exclusive, became against his own will one of the pioneers of modern democracy. When he fought against the sale of indulgences, he abolished the difference between rich and poor. Anyone who wants to can examine his inner self. But when it was a question of indulgences, the rich had a head start on the road to heavenly salvation and the poor could never catch up with them. Now people could be blessed without having a penny in their pocket. "Every Christian who feels genuine repentance," says Luther, "is totally absolved from punishment and guilt without prayers of indulgence."

When he translated the Bible, it became accessible to an entire people. Each person, irrespective of his social standing, could directly and without any intermediaries whatsoever acquire spiritual and moral values. This made modern man, to a notable degree, independent of an external police force and increased his obligation to act in harmony with his inner standards.

The philosophy of existentialism of our day seems to me to some degree to be furthering this way of thought by pointing out that man shapes his life and is forced to make his own choice.

Luther helped to prepare for the conception that inner freedom and personal responsibility are not only a privilege of the few but also a right—and an obligation—for one and all to attain. Without some such basic concept of the individual's right in accord with his own conscience—even against the law —no democracy can function. When the modern democratic constitutions began to guarantee individual rights "that Luther, against his will and intentions, helped secularize, Protestantism made its contribution to a way of life that at times has been uniquely free from fear."

1961

Social Change and the Generation Gap
in a Case of Phobia

I T WOULD BE naïve to think that social progress doesn't cost anything. We know that it costs money. But we are also beginning to see that necessary and worthy reforms may give rise to psychic suffering. Man's ability to adapt to new conditions cannot always keep up with the constant changes in his social environment. This is particularly striking when society is restructured so quickly that the change affects several generations at once.

One of the more gratifying reforms of recent years is the fact that access to higher education has come to depend on the child's talent and not on his parents' income. But this reform in itself may cause misunderstanding and conflict in a home where the parents are inadequately educated while their children go from elementary and junior high school on to high school and college. In a case like this it sometimes happens that the child and his parents no longer speak the same language. Both parents and child are gripped by a sense of loneliness and isolation. Their mutual trust and closeness start to wither and give way to a mutual sense of estrangement.

When as a psychoanalyst you examine this process closely, you find out that children in such homes get the upper hand over their parents intellectually at an early age. There appears a crack in the image they have created of their parents. They easily look down upon and even despise their parents while the early infantile notion of the parents' magical omnipotence stays alive deep inside them. In their fantasy the parents still figure exclusively as sexual beings of monumental proportions and do not undergo the gradual desexualization that is common during the latency period. This is why the child often lives in a constant state of diffuse fear of the threatening parental figures he carries in his unconscious. He also experiences anxiety that his real parents won't be adequate intermediaries between the child himself and the social demands he meets in an environment that the parents are not familiar with and often overrate.

The parents, for their part, avoid setting themselves up as models. When they don't demand to be taken as examples, the children feel they are abandoned to the meaninglessness of life. They lack a clear idea of what is forbidden and what is permitted. The necessary delineation, which would help the child avoid anxiety, is made only partially. The parents' disorientation is heightened by the fact that many of them have themselves moved from a rural environment, with established traditions, into the big city. Their reluctance to serve as authorities for the children is due partially to their own process of social adjustment. In addition, there is the wish (sometimes unrealistic) for their children to go further than they did, for them to become "distinguished." Because of this a very valuable worker and peasant tradition is in danger of fading away during the continuous restructuring of traditional social patterns. The parents stand empty-handed in front of their children and belittle their own significance. Indirectly they educate their children to disobey.

For their part, the children may very early assume a supercilious and arrogant attitude which otherwise is characteristic only of adolescents. A ten-year-old may sometimes have acquired more intellectual knowledge than the parents have succeeded in procuring through their whole lives. The children become authorities for their parents, and not the other way around. They are discouraged from identifying with their parents' social function, professional competence and work ethic, as well as with their responsibility in bringing up a new generation. But if the children do not succeed in identifying with their parents as members of society, we may well wonder somewhat apprehensively if they in turn will grow up to be reliable members of democratic society.

A. Mitscherlich[1] has given a more general reason for the dissociation in the concept of the father's role. His conclusion coincides, by and large, with the view presented above. He says that in our times children no longer experience their father as a teacher because they cannot accompany him to his place of work. They often have a vague idea of what he actually does in his profession. In this way the earlier unity of *Vater als Meister und Vater als Temperament* (father as master and father as temperament) is destroyed, which may in turn lead to emotional disturbances in the child's capacity to learn. But a democracy places great demands on a person's ability to make new experiences and to learn from them, a process which is certainly not restricted to childhood and youth but continues throughout one's life. In the totalitarian states, says Mitscherlich—and as a German psychoanalyst he knows what he is talking about—a person need not whistle more than one tune; all values are directed from above according to a set of fixed norms. Democracy, on the contrary, demands "flexibility and a tolerance of opposition and nonconformity."

In the following I shall try to show how the generation gap contributed to the emergence of a phobic symptom. Insofar as possible, I have let the young man speak for himself, because his conflicts seem representative of many often talented and sensitive young people in similar social situations. His father image which was full of contradictions, his hidden guilt feelings, his somewhat artificial outward gaiety and his diminished tolerance of anxiety had prevented him from giving up his adolescent characteristics. He did not have the courage to take the next step and assume the mature man's sexual and social identity.

A twenty-five-year-old student came for treatment because he had not been able to attend the university during the past year. The building itself caused him to experience an acute sense of terror that he could not overcome. The symptom spread, as usual, and he mostly stayed home, was reluctant to go out and didn't want to meet any people, not even his old friends.

During the first interview I met a young man who had a great deal of boyish charm, a lively intelligence and a disarming smile. He had the relaxed, confident air of today's college students, unrelated to the social background of the person.

Under psychoanalytic treatment the patient at first expressed his positive views on the Nordic forms of democracy: everyone can develop according to his talents; social origin has no relevance. His father had always been a trade-union man and had lived through hard times and unemployment. The young man wasn't politically active but voted along his father's party lines. This position was intellectually acceptable to him. But it was not bound by close emotional ties and was not fully integrated into his personality.

After a while the patient confessed that in high school he hadn't been able to reveal the fact that his father was an ordinary worker. Instead, he made him out to be warehouse foreman. He was ashamed of the cowardice that made him yield to the social snobbery of his class. Most of the pupils lived in a "nicer" part of the city, and their fathers were in relatively high social positions.

The patient forgot to come to the following session and apologized the next day for his negligence. He didn't understand how it could have happened. Still, he remembered a dream he'd had the previous night: "In the dream you are invited home to my parents. You would very much like to meet them and see our apartment. I don't know if I approve or not."

He understood the dream without further comment. He realized that he must look at his background without wishful thinking or euphemism. But the confrontation with reality produced anxiety. His description of his home and also of growing up became the first step toward controlling his constant feeling of anxiety; he tied it down with words.

The patient didn't think that his father was especially talented—he had no formal education. He was a quiet, good-natured man. He used to lose his temper easily, but he also quickly forgot his anger. The father never taught the son anything. When the boy was in elementary school, he already knew more than his father. The son corrected his parents' accent and wanted them to speak in the proper formal manner. He corrected the spelling mistakes in their letters and helped his mother with her housekeeping accounts. But this didn't make him feel triumphant; it only gave him a feeling of hopelessness, slight irritation and regret.

When his father was young he had hurt his leg in an accident. Children on the street used to tease him and call him names when he walked past. Furious and powerless, he ran after them and shook his fist at them. He never caught any of them. They ran faster.

The image of the weak, ridiculed father was reinforced by his mother's attitude. The son was not going to grow up to be like his father. He would become a "distinguished" man with a socially respected situation, and women would be attracted to him, even from a distance. But she misled him also into forging his father's name on a money order. "Of course she needed the money," he said apologetically, "and we told Father about it when he came home in the evening." He didn't like the analyst's silence and added: "Well, Father had nothing against it either." He became restless and confused when the silence persisted.

One day the patient told me quite spontaneously that his father had been a successful wrestler. People had often been afraid of him. He could be merciless when he hit people. He still got into fights easily. They always followed the same pattern: the father emerged victorious and later regretted it. For the first time, the son discovered that even as a grown-up he was mortally afraid of his father's physical strength.

But there was also another father, a father who was neither

helpless nor despised nor terrifyingly brutal. He was a father who had taken care of his little son. He had taken the boy with him on bicycle trips, picked mushrooms with him and taught him to distinguish the different kinds. But this father no longer existed for him. Suddenly the patient became aware of a strange characteristic in his father:

> Father only likes one person at a time. He pays attention to this person and indulges in him. Father ceased to exist for me when I was about six. He came home and was uninterested. But when I visited him at work he glowed. He introduced me to the other workers and to the foreman: "This is my boy."

Now the patient began to realize that at the time his father had focused his attention on his younger brother. Even now he could observe how one-tracked his father's human relationships were in terms of emotion.

It is remarkable how early the young man had dethroned his father, not, as is usually the case, in adolescence, but as early as the age of five or six. The result was that the archaic image of the father, with his monumental physical strength and overwhelming potency, stood unchanged and in sharp contrast to the role his father had as a member of society—and in which he was emotionally undisciplined, a prey of emotionally shifting moods, socially despised and an ignoramus. The positive memory of the father who took care of his son and introduced him in the men's vocational community and in social situations in general was too weakly developed to influence the development of the child's personality structure in any decisive way. Only an impoverished, one-sided picture of the father had remained in his consciousness. This made the son feel lonely and defiant. He experienced this as standing outside society. He was alone against the crowd. He needed no model. He would be able to find his own way of life without asking anyone's advice. In his denial of social obligations, authorities and traditions, we find an expression of his asocial tendencies.

The patient's defense against the hidden image of the terrifying father of his early childhood had emerged as a troublesome characteristic: he provoked people to assault him, partially to overcome the imagined person who was attacking, partially to transform his passivity into action. He denied his identity as a son and made claims to be on the same status as his father. Other people often found him tactless and insolent. He himself had no idea that his irritating and contemptuous behavior made him unpopular among his fellow students and his teachers. They felt that he disturbed the class and was not considerate of others. He was blind to the dislike he encountered and believed that he was popular. The patient became aware of the fact that he had exploited his early intellectual superiority by bluffing his way through and hiding his feeling of physical weakness and general incompetence.

> Actually, I don't want to be a phoney. It was worst in school— to keep up that attitude. I made it through with my phenomenal memory. I knew all kinds of technical terms. I could juggle expressions around, be "learned" on the surface. Now I'm afraid to sit down and drink a cup of coffee with people, afraid they'll find out I'm a phoney. I've acted strong, big, and inaccessible—you can't isolate yourself. I was weak—no good in fights. Physically I was ill-equipped. I talked people down. Mama said: "You shouldn't fight, the way Papa does. You can always talk things over." I beat them intellectually. And then they didn't attack. The more insecure I get, the more I curse and use catch-words, acting stuck-up. If you're weak physically, you use language to get the upper hand. I could get the best of Father intellectually, but I never won out over him physically. I was in command of him intellectually. I murdered him—well, I wouldn't say that. When I was a kid, I was more on his intellectual than physical level.

Now he realized that his earlier reactive activity, restlessness and anxiety covered a feeling of deep insufficiency. In his heart he doubted that he would be able to do anything at all that was responsible and sustained. Now he did everything as if "making believe," without learning anything thoroughly. For the first time he had the courage to experience the abyss of shame and self-hatred he had been carrying about inside him. A dream revealed both his defense by means of provocation and his anxious fear of being annihilated by his father.

> I was playing in an orchestra. The teacher was also present. He accused me of playing the wrong melody. I answered fast as lightning: "I'm not the one who's doing it—you are!"
>
> Two men were coming toward me. One of them pressed his knee against my back. I saw his eyes. I knew that he was serious. I saw him pick up a steel bar and swing it at me, an instrument of torture.

The patient woke up with an acute sense of anxiety. Suddenly he realized that it was exactly the same anguish he felt toward the university building. Then he said thoughtfully: "Father doesn't like my being an academic. He thinks that I should have become a worker like he was."

After this the patient started to wish for a kind of companionship with his father. He was aware that he needed him for his own social orientation and without guilt admitted that he would have preferred a father who acted as a guide for him. A dream indicated his effort at reorientation which was also apparent in his somewhat resigned narration:

> It was like having a nightmare while you're awake. When I was in school and took my comprehensive exams, I heard the same old argument constantly: "Then all doors will be open to you!" It turned out to be quite the opposite, exactly the other way around. Last night I dreamed that I was out on a flat plain. I saw children leaving home to go to school. I followed them. I entered a house through a long corridor. A door was ajar. The room was cold. Bearded, white old men were sitting at a long table. I stopped . . . stared, and made a fool of myself. I went out again. The old ones only laughed. I saw it as it ought to have been: I should have been little and should have followed one of the men and been introduced by him. I would have been protected, and they'd have had me study something. You can be introduced very peacefully and quietly. Very simply be with someone. Once I went with Father to a chess club. I liked it. But he never wanted to play chess with me. Nowadays I decline all invitations to enter through the open door.

But one day I will have to step in, even if there's no old man who'll be able to introduce me. I have equipped myself with knowledge in order to go in, and I've thought that I have everything those old men have. Maybe I've tried to compensate for one failing and another by means of knowledge. When you are little and sitting next to an old grandfather, you get it for free. When I'll enter, it won't be to become one of them, nor to be accepted. But now that's wrong! The message has to be passed on! First you have to be accepted as a candidate. At that point the old people lead. They won't get angry if I'm an utter failure. They'll only say very calmly: "We're sorry, it's unfortunate, but it's impossible." I continued only through the dark corridor—I never entered—and stepped outside at the other end. The sun was shining there once again. I should have gone on studying instead of giving in to this anguish. I hesitated. I never went again. At that time I wanted something. Now I don't desire anything in particular. Naturally I want to work, but I don't have the courage. Am I afraid of him? Do I want to protect my body from him? I don't know if he likes me. I would so much like to ask. I don't know how to ask someone who's older, someone who knows more. I want so much to ask. In the past I didn't give a damn about the teachers and all the other so-called authorities. I thought I knew everything myself. But how—how the hell do you ask? . . . "Excuse me?"

Both the choice of the theme and the setting in this dream correspond amazingly well with some of the key episodes in Kafka's novel *The Trial*. My patient was not familiar with the story, in which K., a young man, searches in vain for his judge.

After a struggle the patient managed to come up with a fundamental insight: If a person has not learned as a child to ask his father about something he doesn't know, then it will be difficult for him later on to ask his teachers for help. At that point he developed an expressed need to be allowed to revive his father and overcome all the unspoken antagonism that had existed between them. After several weeks he told me joyfully that his father had asked him if he wanted to share the car with him. He was afraid to say yes, but he was proud that his father wished to be friends with him. He recounted this episode several times during the subsequent sessions, as if it were a completely new event that he wanted to tell me about. But it did not seem that he had revised his notion of his father. While in the past he had spoken disparagingly of his father's clumsiness in handling a radio, a TV set and a motorcycle, he now was proud to be accepted by him in the technical field.

Only then did he remember a minor episode that had occurred shortly before his breakdown. One morning on his way to the university he had passed some men who were repairing the street. Suddenly he was struck by a yearning to be able to work alongside them. He had wanted to get off the bus at the next stop and ask the men if they had any work for him. But he hadn't done it. He had remained in his seat as if paralyzed. Several days later his phobia had appeared and put an end to the fellowship he shared with the students and teachers he knew at the university.

To his surprise, this promising young student discovered that in a very subdued way he despised academic people. He considered intellectual work a luxury, something that wasn't really essential. Only a person who worked with his body accomplished something essential, something of general use. In other words, his choice of profession had led him into an unresolvable conflict. The son, who could not accept his father wholeheartedly because he was "merely" an uneducated worker, secretly despised himself because he "just sat and read books." He had enrolled at the university not only because he was bright and had a genuine interest in his field, but also because he unconsciously felt that he was too weak and frail to be a manual laborer. But now he was caught in an unresolvable dilemma. Consciously he refused to identify with his father's positive tradition as a representative of the working class and as the breadwinner of the family. But unconsciously he had accepted the negative tradition. He shared his father's prejudices.

Ultimately, on his own initiative, the patient formed a moral stand that was as simple as it was valid and that bridged the tense relations between the generations: "You said that I should work. I thought you meant get a job. But suddenly it dawned on me that studying is work, too."

He had become reconciled with his father and was now on

equal terms with him. Both had a socially acceptable function: they worked in order to earn a living. The kind of work they did was less important.

On the basis of extensive observations the American psychoanalyst Peter Bloss[2] has argued that young people have an undeniable need for continuity. What might on the surface seem like a neurotic reaction appears upon closer examination to be an attempt to establish ties between the past and the planned future. Bloss gives an example of a talented young man who suddenly abandoned his university studies in order to live among workers. He was an adopted child and had grown up in an orderly academic environment. His relationship with his foster parents had been good. But through his second year he had lived with a working-class family who had liked him very much. The young man's apparent neurotic behavior, for which he himself could give no explanation because he lacked conscious memories of that time, proved to be an effort to create a continuity between two forms of life. He was at home among the workers. When he understood that they had accepted him, he was able to return to the foster home and continue his studies.

My patient had not given in to his impulse to get off the bus and work alongside the men on the street. Instead, he acquired a phobia which gave rise to an insurmountable block between his past and his present. The neurotic symptom forced him to realize that he had not succeeded in giving his life a sense of continuity. Under psychoanalytic treatment he was obliged to recognize his illness and fundamentally to redirect his own existence. His constant desire to know the truth about himself and to find a worthwhile place in the adult world became his best ally when he was struggling against a wordless anxiety that time and again threatened to annihilate him totally.

Franz Kafka's father was a man whose frightening muscular strength silenced the son and forced on him a sense of physical inferiority throughout his life. "Your threat ('Don't talk back to me'), with raised hand, has followed me constantly," he wrote bitterly when he was an adult. Without any illusions at all Kafka realized that he was not capable of achieving the mature man's natural self-assurance. Resigned, he said of himself: "A human being who has been cheated of his childhood and who all the same always remains an adolescent, inside and out—dragged on somewhat slowly from the previous generation."

In terms of general cultural orientation, it is difficult to imagine a gap wider than the one that separated Herman Kafka (1852–1934) and his son, Franz (1883–1924). Herman Kafka was the son of a dirt-poor Jewish working-class family in rural Czechoslovakia. When he was ten years old he became a door-to-door peddler. People mocked and chased him as he drew his cart from one rich peasant farm to another. At twenty he made his way to the big city, Prague, obsessed by one single fanatical idea: his child would not go through the same social contempt that he himself had suffered. His son would get the best education and be admitted to "refined" (that is to say, German-speaking) circles.

Herman Kafka's intention was more than fulfilled. Not only did Franz Kafka become a doctor of law at the University of Prague, he also became an influential innovator in German prose. But the refined, extremely withdrawn, melancholy young man tried in vain to achieve a harmonious relationship with his boorish, dominating and often inconsiderate father. Finally Franz Kafka became his own judge, more cruel and merciless than his father ever had been. (*Cf.* Harry Järv, *Varaktigare än koppar* ["More Durable Than Copper"] [Malmö Cavefors, 1962].)

The First Love of Youth—and of Childhood

When a poet is asked about his first love,
he thinks of being in love as a teenager—
a psychoanalyst thinks of his mother.

A CCORDING to Freud all cultural change and development is based on the dynamic interplay between successive generations. It is the essential task of puberty to bring about this change. Incestuous fantasies gradually fade away and the emotional detachment from parental authority grows.

Because of the increasingly complicated structure of modern mass society, this process is no longer confined to puberty but lasts through the whole period of adolescence, which generally passes into adulthood around the age of twenty-five. This prolonged period of personality growth is now the subject of much interest on the part of researchers. Important studies have been made on the transformation of superego and ego ideals and on the development of a new identity, out of which the new equilibrium—characteristic of the adult—emerges.

Since psychoanalytic research is based mainly on the study of single individuals, the psychoanalyst may not always be aware of the importance this newly acquired identity of young people has for the continuity of Western culture. The specific integration of traditional and modern values which each generation has to accomplish in adolescence fills the gap between the past and the future. It is an obligation to the past as well as to the future. But in time the militant new ego ideals of young people will be passed on to their children and are bound to become the superego of the coming generations.

It is worth mentioning that the *content* of the superego varies far more readily than its actual *tone of voice*. The superego can have the same tone, gentle or strict, through several generations, but a totally different content. The father of a woman patient had been brought up in the rigid, authoritarian environment of the Baltic aristocracy before the First World War. He hated their arrogance, especially their contempt for the poor. As a young man he emigrated to Sweden and adopted views fervently in support of trade unionism. When his daughter once called the housekeeper *"piga"* (maid), she got a severe spanking. As a grown-up, she denounced her father's trade unionism and developed more moderate ideals. But she imposed these on her own children with a severity similar to that of her trade-unionist father and aristocratic grandfather.

The young person's new, personally acquired superego and ego ideals[1] are invested with a great deal of narcissistic libido.[2] They are his *raison d'être,* his ticket of admission into the adult world. They are the bulwark that prevents the young person from losing his identity and from once again falling back uncritically to the unchanged modes of life of his elders: "My father did, so why shouldn't I?" The dreams and goals of adolescence are defenses which belong, as the American analyst Gitelson has said, "to the building blocks of human character at its highest potential."[3]

A halfhearted, pessimistic attitude toward the ideals of a person's youth and their eventual sacrifice can result in serious personality disturbances in people between the ages of forty and fifty. They have come to an emotional dead end—often in spite of considerable outward success. The serious loss of the narcissistic libido which has been invested in their goals and ideals leads to a feeling of self-contempt and an attitude of cynical destructiveness. The immortal demand of Marquis Posa in Schiller's play *Don Carlos*—"*Sagen Sie ihm dass er vor den Träumen seiner Jugend Achtung haben soll, wenn er Mann sein wird*"[4] ("Tell him that he shall have to respect the dreams of his youth if he wants to become a man")—is well-founded mental-hygiene counseling to preserve the self-esteem and the personal dignity of adults.

The capacity to retain the ideas of your youth throughout life with undiminished intensity and freshness seems to be an outstanding characteristic of great men, who in this respect remain eternally young. Isaiah Berlin[5] maintains that this was true of the founder of the state of Israel, Chaim Weizmann, whose biography he has written.

During his entire life Weizmann felt the unrelenting obligation of his youth to identify "with some living force in the world and to take part in the world's affairs with all the risk of blame and misinterpretation and misunderstanding of one's motives and character which this almost invariably entails."[6]

In his famous paper[7] on the limitations of democracy, Judge Learned Hand describes the dilemma of the modern voter who knows how impossible it is to form a sound opinion of the complicated affairs of the modern state. Adults often turn away from any participation in it and go about their own business. But the voice of his personal superego makes him feel uneasy: "I'm aware of those protests of my youth lingering in my memory, calling upon me to gird up my loins and fall to."

When we speak of ideals, a Norwegian writer once said, we always mean the ideals of youth. They last our whole life.

The relative stability of the goals we have acquired in adolescence stands in striking contrast to the constant change and oscillations of the ways and means we use to reach them. While the goals are constant, the means vary in the history of a generation as well as in that of an individual. A historic example of this is afforded by the Norwegian conscientious objectors of the 1920s and 1930s. They were a rather large group of young intellectuals who, in spite of their former refusal to use force, were the first to participate in the war against the German invaders in 1940, in order to protect their ideals of democracy and freedom.

While fixed goals are desirable and give life a uniform orientation, clinging stubbornly to the same means can be disastrous. A relatively mature adult should remain loyal to his ideals, but at the same time be able to change the means of realizing them. Only a mature person is able to combine a stability of goals with flexibility in the choice of appropriate means.

From the psychoanalytic point of view, the establishment of new goals can be considered a result of ego-syntonic displacements. This confirms the fact that adolescence is the phase of life in which the individual develops a surprising ability to sublimate. The means and methods, in short, the techniques for achieving results, vary according to the quickly shifting balance between the neutralized instinctual energy[8] and the uncontrolled, impulsive acts of adolescence. In this period of life the strange tension between relatively firm aims and abruptly changing ways of reaching them explains the marked unreliability—and the irresistible charm—of young people. The well-known disillusionment of youth originates not only in the degradation of the internalized parental figures, but also in not knowing how to reach the newly acquired goals. Lacking a sense of distance to new and old goals and grappling with temporary uncontrolled instinctual breakthroughs, the adolescent doesn't have an opportunity to develop smooth and flexible techniques and methods. He tries to reach the stars but fails, not least because his techniques are often unrealistic, shortsighted and aggressive.

A young man who was a devoted world federalist became very angry when I once called him an idealist. "It's only a practical question of approximately four or five years before we have a universal federation of all countries and a world government." (This was said in 1952.)

There are many reasons for the well-known impatience of youth. Lack of appropriate distance for the newly established aims of life is only one. The impatient fervor and the heightened intensity of life are also the outcome of a sociobiological change. Man's perennial biological helplessness, which Freud regarded as one cause for the development of neurosis, is overcome, together with social dependence. The new feeling of body strength and the prospect of social independence produce decisive changes in the individual's balance between activity and passivity. The wish to give back what you have received leads—as Wittels[9] has pointed out in his excellent study of adolescence— to an astonishing generosity which fills the older generation with nostalgic envy. Never again in his life will the individual experience the same unlimited capacity for devotion and self-sacrifice as in adolescence. Biological and social maturity enforce the drive to identify[10] actively and establish one's own goals.

It seems as if the magic desire for omnipotence could be realized. This feeling of biological strength enables the young person to stand up against the pressure of tradition, to choose what to keep and what to discard. It is a process of continuous trial and error until finally a balance is reached.

The increasing independence and the newly acquired ideals inspire the adolescent to develop the illusion of "free will." A young person is tormented, sometimes even paralyzed, by the growing insight that he has to make a choice here and now; otherwise life will pass away from him and he will have lost his chance, once and for all. A depressive sense of tragedy and meaninglessness changes suddenly into a feeling of joy and elation when he is convinced that he has now found his role in life. The ambivalence of youth, which Wittels mentions as the first phase of adolescence, gives the search the characteristic mixture of self-debasement and boundless pride. In the no-man's-land between childhood and the adult world the adolescent thinks like young Frédéric, Flaubert's hero: "I belong to the race of the disinherited; I could just as well embrace a treasure of artificial gems as one of diamonds."[11]

Time and again psychoanalytic writers—first and foremost Anna Freud[12]—have pointed out the difficulties of analyzing patients in the age of puberty and adolescence. Because of the patient's needs, the psychoanalyst has constantly to alter his methods, as K. Eisler has described. Temporary solutions may seem permanent not only to the patient but occasionally even to the analyst. That is why it seems—as so often in the development of psychoanalysis—to be so useful when treating an adult to scrutinize the patient's youth and its influence on his personality structure.

In contrast to the experiences of childhood, the experiences of adolescence are easily remembered in the analysis. Very often the patient looks back at this phase of his life with a sense of relief: at least he has done something on his own to overcome his early conflicts. This makes it easier for him to accept the help of another person. The analyst becomes the symbol of his active effort to find—or to regain—the inner meaning of his life and to work through those childhood conflicts he had attempted to resolve. If the analyst doesn't give the patient credit for having found some solutions on his own, or at least for having tried to do so, if he rejects all the patient's endeavors as insufficient and unrealistic, he can risk an impoverishment of the ego and an increase of passive, dependent attitudes in the transference situation.

Moreover, it seems to me that childhood conflicts in general are not accessible to analysis without a thorough understanding of the processes of identification and displacement which occurred during adolescence and of the new equilibrium which emerged through the regrouping of defensive attitudes.[13]

The experience of treating adults gives the impression that the adolescent is rarely able to solve basic instinctual and emotional conflicts. But this ego is provided with new opportunities to cope with them through the increasing psychobiological independence, the transformation of the superego and ego ideals, the change in aims, the elaboration of new techniques to reach them and a new balance between instinctual and neutralized energy.

Just as the superego during the latency period is an heir to the infantile Oedipus constellation,[14] the first love of youth seems to have a similarly decisive function. The new love object not only indicates the final displacement—or as Katan[15] calls it "removal"—of the incestuous object choice but often also provides an important impulse toward a transformation in the superego and ego ideals as well as in the awareness of a new identity. These first loves of youth owe a good deal of their special fascination to the sudden, intense revival of some special phase in the infantile Oedipus constellation. Very often these first love objects are given up and a new type representing another phase of the Oedipus constellation is chosen and becomes permanent.

The first of the following cases shows how changes in the balance of activity and passivity in adolescence caused the patient to gain insight into his illness when later in life under special stress this balance was threatened. The other cases show that the whole Oedipus constellation is not reactivated in adolescence but only special phases of its development, as the number of successive objects of youthful love indicates. A study of the first loves in all these cases indicates that the process of displacement and the transformation of ego ideals can take place while the underlying instinctual conflict remains unsolved or only partly solved.

Furthermore, all the cases point to an unresolved conflict between ends and means due to a tension between the stability of displacements and the instability of action. They all reveal a disturbance of the interplay between structure and function, as Heinz Hartmann[16] has described.

The first case shows how the achievements of adolescence (the irreversible choice of a heterosexual love object and the ego ideal of an active, mature woman) counteracted regression to a passive dependency on a complicated mother image and the threat of latent homosexual urges breaking through.

A thirty-two-year-old married woman, mother of three children, had for the past three or four years suffered from depressions, extreme fatigue and increasing apathy. This culminated in an acute, dramatic breakdown with heart attacks, violent crying and a diffuse anxiety that something terrible might happen. After the patient had become relatively calm, her physician recommended psychoanalytic treatment. She accepted the advice with a sense of relief. She felt this was an opportunity to recapture her former active, gay, lively personality.

During the first period of her treatment the patient talked mostly about her adolescent years: how she had acquired emotional and social independence. She had even been able to give considerable support to her family. During this phase of life she had also developed many interests—literary, social and political. She remembered her active role in youth clubs and how happy she had been when she met her present husband. Looking back on these years, she was surprised to notice her ability to make friends and to communicate with the most diverse people.

As a child her behavior had been quite different. She had often been sad and shy. It never occurred to her that she might have rights of her own. Whatever care she got was pure mercy. She could neither expect nor ask for anything.

A tragic family constellation had pushed her into the position of the unwanted child. Her mother had married a foreigner, who in spite of intensive work never succeeded in attaining economic stability. The family was occasionally supported by a female relative of the mother, a vigorous, domineering person who ruled the family. The father had abdicated. At home he was silent, not unfriendly but remote. In later years he began to drink rather heavily. The mother was not only economically, but above all emotionally, dependent on her relative, with a mixture of love and hate, open fear and hidden resentment. Looking back on this relationship, the patient realized with increasing uneasiness the strong homosexual bond that existed between the two women and their outspoken contempt for men.

The elderly relative never forgave the mother for marrying a foreigner. The mother's life was dominated by a constant effort to please the woman and to atone for the fact that she had dared marry against her will. The woman didn't like children, so the mother's load of guilt increased when the first child, a son, was born. He developed into a tyrannical, spoiled youngster; guilt feelings toward this child, which her relative had begrudged her, made the mother yield to all his demands. Nobody was pleased when she became pregnant the second time. The father worried about the increase in economic responsibility; the elderly lady, who considered children a nuisance, blamed her for "carelessness." Of course, the little son wasn't pleased either. Why should he have a sister, he who was the center of the family? From birth on, the little girl was assigned the role of an intruder. In childhood the feeling that nobody wanted her hovered over her like a dark cloud. Her mother forced her to obey the relative blindly, otherwise she would be angry with the mother and start reproaching her for having had another child. The woman treated her like a funny little plaything, completely at her disposal. The brother retained an attitude of superiority toward the girl. Her mother used to tell her that neither she nor her father had really wanted her. But when she was born, they had been very happy. The child felt that the mother told the truth: no one had longed for her, but nevertheless her mother did love her, with a sad, resigned and nostalgic affection. Her father could be kind to her, too, sing her the songs of his homeland and give her small presents. But he didn't take part in educating her. He left this to the two women, who never asked for his opinion. Later on, when he began to drink, the girl considered it a sign of his suppressed hatred for the women in the family.

Her mother's example taught the patient how to suffer with dignity and to enjoy the hidden gratification of martyrdom. Very early she learned to blame herself for her desperate longing for a carefree, gay life and to suppress her wish for an active father figure. In adolescence external circumstances and internal insecurity prevented her from fighting for her right to have an adequate education. When she was nineteen, she took a job in an office and supported herself. She was no longer the intruder now. On the contrary, she succeeded in becoming a considerable help to her family. This filled her with pride and stabilized her self-esteem, which as a child had been below zero, as she herself expressed it. But a slight feeling of unease at having had the development of her inner qualities restricted never quite left her.

Moreover, the little intruder had suddenly discovered the surprising fact that she had grown into an attractive young woman. She was surrounded by quite a few young men who made her realize that she played an important role in their lives. Gradually she overcame her shyness. Her body posture changed. The little girl who had always gazed down at the floor, who had constantly been scolded for her stooping shoulders, suddenly straightened up. She began to enjoy her body; her posture became erect and proud. Now, at last, she became a person in her own right, someone people had to take into account.

Rather early in life she met a shy young man who had a modest job. She immediately sensed his great capacity for devotion and loyalty and admired his clear and detached judgment. They fell in love and soon married, against the will of her parents. The young woman decided to do all she could to give her husband the power and authority her father had never possessed. She succeeded only partly. Her husband had a brilliant and rapid professional career. Their economic standard was markedly higher than that of her parents. But the young man did not assume his authority within the family, which in several years had increased with three children. Instead, he displayed an ambivalent dependence on his own mother, who gradually invaded the family. She began to take over the household duties and tried to gain authority over the children by openly and extremely disloyally competing with their mother. The two women quarreled constantly. The worried husband didn't know what to do, torn between mother and wife by his loyalty to both. He tried to remain neutral and began to spend most of his leisure time outside the home.

In a strange way, the patient was back in the family constellation of her childhood. All that she had achieved in her youth, her successful fight against identification with her submissive mother, her rehabilitation of the father in the form of her husband, her reversal from shy and clinging dependence to active dominance—everything was in danger. The widening gap between her aims in life and the sad reality of her present situation made her desperate. To give up the ideals of her youth would mean suicide—a fantasy that had now and then occurred to her during the recent years.

But the patient also felt guilty because of her revolt. She wondered if it hadn't been her duty to submit to the tyranny of her mother-in-law, just as her own mother had accepted the domination of an older woman. Perhaps she should accept her husband's neutrality and understand, once and for all, that men cannot be expected to take an active part in family life. Perhaps she was now going to be punished for her decision to live a more worthy life than her mother. Finally she collapsed in the anxiety attack mentioned before.

Looking back on the analysis of this patient, we see that she reacted with anxiety and depression when her newly acquired identity was threatened. When she was a child she almost completely identified with her humble, suffering mother, but she succeeded in modifying this identification by integrating special aspects of her older relative and a sister of her father. From the former she acquired an active, unsentimental attitude toward life, while the latter, a happily married woman, showed her that it was possible to take care of a big family and at the same time actively take part in the political and social work of the community. The balance in the configuration which emerged in adolescence was threatened when the constellation in the patient's own family overlapped with that of her childhood. Her identity pattern fell apart because of an unsolved infantile conflict. If she identified completely with her mother, she risked her independent position in the family and her role as an attractive woman. She would destroy herself just as her mother had once destroyed her own beauty. She would cease to please men and demonstrate her contempt by neglecting her appearance. She would submit to her mother-in-law and gratify her latent homosexual urges. From puberty on, she had tried to master these by reaction formation, the changed pattern of her basic identification and her heterosexual ego ideals, which were in conscious contrast to those of her mother. She had kept her ideals, but she no longer knew how to live up to them because of the aggressive and self-destructive tendencies that threatened to emerge.

This patient was constantly analyzed from two points of view: the uncovering of childhood memories and the way in which she had tried to solve the conflict in adolescence. The wish to regain what she had lost was the driving force in her recovery.

The transference of the heterosexual love object (father) to the new object (husband) remained stable throughout the crisis and the psychoanalytic treatment. She never doubted that she had made the right choice in life.

The stable choice of love object during adolescence, which is characteristic of this patient, seems nevertheless to be an exception. Usually adolescence is marked by a continuous trial-and-error period in choosing new love objects. Often the first love of youth, which represents the image of the fully developed Oedipus situation, is given up in favor of a secondary one, representing a later phase. The latter choice not only indicates an omission of fear and guilt, but also satisfies latent homosexual urges by means of narcissistic identification. If the resignation which is always tied to this choice is fully accepted by the ego, the choice may lead to stable relationships throughout life. Even though the memory of the first love of youth leaves a faint tinge of nostalgia, it is recognized clearly as incompatible with the new life of the adult. But when full and lasting resignation is not achieved, the secondary love object will consciously or unconsciously be blamed for not being like the "real" first one. Just as the beloved brother of the little girl can never fulfill all the requirements made of a powerful father figure, the man who represents the secondary love object will always remind the grown-up woman that there was once another man who gave the promise of greater fulfillment. The ideals and the style of life she had acquired in relation to her first love in adolescence may not come true in the later relationship and may cause an insoluble conflict.

A thirty-eight-year-old woman teacher was married to a scholar two years younger than she. They had three children. She came for treatment because occasionally she couldn't control the feelings of defiance she felt raging inside her. She didn't want to hurt anyone, and also she knew that making a scene wouldn't get her anywhere. But she couldn't resist doing it. She felt that everything had gone wrong when she married her present husband. Although he had a good income, she couldn't always rely on him as far as money was concerned. Every time he spent too much, he expected her to help him. He made friends with people who didn't deserve his friendship and was easily exploited by people who flattered him. He had a lot of boyish charm that she couldn't resist. He would suddenly scold her for something unimportant, and the next minute overwhelm her with tenderness. The husband's family also were emotionally somewhat unstable. Despite their good economic situation, their cultural level was low. Their way of life had no taste or style.

The patient's parents were still alive. Time after time she appealed to them to support her right to keep a certain distance from her husband and his family. But, each time, her parents asked her to remain steadfast no matter how her husband and his family behaved. She hoped they would finally understand her, instead they coldly repudiated her, and she felt she had been abandoned and treated unjustly. This otherwise very mature and intelligent woman couldn't stop thinking that one day her parents, especially her mother, would fully acknowledge all she had had to endure in her marriage.

During the analysis she constantly returned to her carefree, happy life before the war when she was studying at an English university. There she had met her real true love. She had become engaged to a wealthy older lawyer from a well-known and respected family. He had been a confident, lively and domineering man with a certain sense of humor and some psychological insight. He had admired her intelligence, her good judgment and her desire to understand the patterns of behavior in her new environment. But in one way or another he had always succeeded in getting his way in such a considerate and unassuming way that the patient had been able to accept it without feeling defeated. Then the war broke out. Her parents had sent her a telegram telling her to come home immediately. Her fiancé had wanted her to stay where she was and to marry him at once. After a short, desperate struggle, she had gone back home. After that, she had really started having difficulties. "Since then, I've never been myself."

After a short while she had lost touch with her fiancé. Soon after this, she had married the young scholar. She had been fully aware of his emotional instability but had been attracted to his charming sensuality and his good-naturedness. She had also been conscious of the difference in their respective families as far as cultural background and social position were concerned, although she had tried to dismiss this as unimportant.

In analyzing her motivation for this fateful decision, different sides of her Oedipal constellation were revealed.

The patient had grown up in an aristocratic family. During her childhood and youth she had experienced a decline in their social prestige and changes in their style of life resulting from the industrialization in her native country. The number of servants had diminished steadily. More and more rooms in their big house had been closed. The father had no longer been able to order his workers around; he'd had to negotiate with them. From being rulers in a little kingdom, her parents—although they were still wealthy—had become ordinary citizens in a modern industrial state. The parents, of course, had felt bitter at their loss of prestige. So had the daughter. Secretly she hadn't been able to forgive her father for having permitted himself to be dethroned. He should have been more despotic. Her mother also had blamed the father for having forced her into a situation in which she had to assume the daily duties of a middle-class housewife. In their bitterness toward the father, the mother and daughter had joined forces against him. Very early in life the mother had considered her daughter a confidential friend. She had been entrusted with the care of her brother, who was five years younger than she, and she had been made responsible for his schooling. When he wasn't making any progress in school, it had always been her fault: she hadn't quizzed him on his homework properly.

Only in her youth, away from her family and in completely new surroundings, did the patient start questioning whether her mother had been right in giving her such a considerable responsibility. At a moment of happiness she had suddenly felt that now it was her turn to look forward and make something of her own life. Her engagement to the older man illustrated her efforts to free herself from a masochistic dependence on her mother. Her father, who had been dethroned both externally and internally, had been rehabilitated in her choice of a man who represented real power in modern society. She had overcome her *ressentiment* toward the new form of society by combining in her own personal life-style a view of the old and the new upper-class existence. Her ego ideal had changed radically. Self-discipline and personal dignity, an unfaltering sense of authenticity —in relation to both people and things—and a growing understanding of the necessity to be socially responsible had become the values that, from this point on, were clearly laid down for her. By living up to these ideals she had discovered her self-respect. She had found a group of people whom she felt confortable with. When she had yielded to the demand of her parents, she had given up her fiancé, who represented the powerful father figure of childhood, but her newly acquired ideals remained. After this her sexual desires were directed toward a secondary love object, her brother, whom she had both loved and hated. Now she served her husband in the same way she had once served her brother. She was once again obeying her mother's demands. In the meantime she could never forget that she had once in her life met a man who had given her much more than her husband could ever give. Unconsciously she could never forgive her husband for not being a substitute for her father. In the course of the treatment, her bitterness and her hidden guilt feelings over the fact that she didn't love him enough diminished. Gradually she found a way of living within the framework of her marriage.

It sometimes happens that psychoanalytic treatment comes to a standstill until some events of adolescence are worked out. In general these events are not inaccessible. But the patient depreciates them and looks mockingly and shamefully back at the "sins and stupidities of his youth."

In the following case a considerable displacement in the incestuous object choice was given up. As a result, the personality level became lower, obsessional attitudes appeared and special ego ideals were denied. After a period of extreme ambivalence, at the onset of maturity a stability of the personality and ego ideals was achieved, although on a somewhat lower level.

Shortly after the war, a forty-year-old German political refugee came to therapy because he couldn't find a solution to his current conflict: should he go back to Germany or stay in the country where he had become a citizen? He was married to a Swedish woman, somewhat older than himself, whom he had met in his new homeland. They had two children.

During the first interview the patient said he suffered from nightmares: a bear was standing motionless at the bedside, and he woke up terrified with the feeling that there was something dark and threatening in the room.

In the first phase of analysis the patient began to understand that his wife represented his older sister, his father's favorite, and on a deeper level the father himself. She was a professional woman, firm, intelligent and kind. The patient had a tendency to maneuver her into situations in which she had to play a dominant role.

Despite the patient's growing insight into his unconscious homosexual conflicts, his actual situation didn't change much. He still didn't know whether he would go back or not. He gave the impression of a record that was stuck. The patient himself was aware that he was moving in a circle.

Once he mentioned incidentally, with a little laugh, that as a young student he had fallen in love with a real German Gretchen. If her father hadn't intervened, he might have married her. "Imagine me, married to a woman whose thoughts were concerned with *Kirche, Küche, Kinder*" (church, kitchen and children). To his surprise, I said I could very well imagine it.

While the patient's memories had till then centered around childhood events, he now began to look back at himself as a young student in an idyllic German university town. He remembered his wanderings in the surrounding countryside, the blue hills on the horizon, the river winding its silvery ribbon through green meadows. He began to long for the early soft beginning of springtime in southern Germany and felt gloomy and chilly at the dramatic display of the cold beauty of the Nordic spring. The two contrasting experiences of spring, although realistic, also symbolized—as became apparent later on —the patient's relation to two totally different feminine ideals: the German mother and the Swedish wife.

He remembered how he had loved the romantic poets and what Eichendorff, Novalis and Hölderlin had meant to him. He talked about his activities in the German youth movement, which for a short while had brought him rather close to the mentality of the Nazis. The young girl he had fallen in love with was sweet, innocent and kindhearted. Her lack of intelligence and her indolence didn't bother him. At night he used to sing German folksongs beneath her window. These serenades enraged the girl's father. He threatened to report the troubadour to the police for trespassing.

When he was describing this, the patient suddenly began to wonder why this threat had made him retire immediately. He didn't try to speak to the girl any more or write an explanatory letter. Several months later he moved to another university, where he finished his studies. Soon he had forgotten the whole episode.

After this experience a change took place in his personality. He gave up his flirtation with the reactionary youth movement. He understood that it had been no more than a childish revolt against his father, a man of moderate socialist opinions. Now he became far more radical than his father and joined a group on the extreme left. After a while the growing power of the Nazis forced him to revise his political opinions again. He began to appreciate the significance of moderation, patience and tolerance as opposed to the violent terror of the Nazis. He returned to his father's more liberal views, though transformed by the experiences of his own generation.

Now the patient began to realize that a general emotional impoverishment had followed the change in his political opinions. He had lost his interest in art and literature. He no longer enjoyed nature. He had become afraid of spontaneous judgments. He distrusted his own likes and dislikes. He was afraid of the blindness of love. He had chosen a wife—he thought—because they worked in the same field and had common political interests.

When the patient regained contact with his personality as a young man, several changes occurred. It started with a little incident. One day he came to his usual session somewhat embarrassed, excusing himself for his tie. When I asked what was wrong with it, he answered, still more embarrassed: "I haven't worn a light blue tie for 20 years. I'm certainly too old to wear light colors."

His nightmares became worse. Finally the bear proved to be the powerful father of his early childhood. Now he was able to remember his incestuous feelings toward his mother and the overpowering fear of being punished by the castrating father. He began to see the connection between the young Gretchen and his mother. Both had been warm, domestic and unpretentious women who never tried to interfere with the political and social affairs of men. His current conflict, whether or not he should go back to his native country, was unconsciously a conflict between two types of women: the mother-Gretchen of his youth and the sister-wife of the new country, where he now had his roots.

For the third time in his life the patient was confronted by a special Oedipus situation. In childhood the fear of castration had forced him to give up his primal love object and to return to the inverted Oedipus constellation. For a short time in adolescence he had succeeded in overcoming his fear of castration and transferring the mother image to a young girl. Again he couldn't maintain this position. Latent homosexual drives, mobilized by the fear of castration, made him give up the first love of his youth and later on choose a less dangerous love object, the sister. His inner equilibrium was now stabilized, though it had compulsive characteristics. This stability was threatened again when, at a later age, he had to make a decision of great importance to his and his wife's common future.

Adolescence had left the patient with a conflict between emotions that were bound to ideals he no longer accepted, on the one hand, and a sensible insight into and evaluation of the present, on the other hand. His analysis led to a reconciliation between the sentiments of adolescence and the adult's sober judgment of facts.

The last case tries to follow the transformation of the personality structure in its nascent state. In many respects it seems to illustrate Heinz Hartmann's statement that "what started in a situation of conflict may secondarily become part of the non-conflictual sphere."[17] It depicts the decisive change from a state of passive dependence to an active giving out during the transformation of childhood identifications into the final identity of the grown-up.

Because of the sudden death of his father, a young man of twenty had become the head of a large company. For some years he ran the business rather successfully, yet he remained dissatisfied with his own life. He felt forced into a career that wasn't his own. He had yielded to his mother's wish to see him and herself well established in a secure social and economic position.

At the age of twenty-five he decided to leave the company and to devote himself to studies that his mother condemned as being a "luxury." He moved to another city and began to study literature and art. He came for treatment because he was tormented by doubts as to whether he had made the right choice. Maybe his mother was right when she wanted him to make money in a high position and live without facing economic troubles. Or was he right in choosing a career—evidently not quite so honorable—which would never bring him the same social and economic standing as his father had had?

It was easy to discern that the patient's fear of not being able to live up to the image of an active and successful father played an important part in his decision to break with the environment of his childhood. He felt his father had never helped him become a real boy. Bitterly he remembered how his father had talked about the little boy's small hands and sweet face "just as if they were made of porcelain." His education was left entirely up to the mother. She dominated him with her constant worries and her apparent weakness. The son always felt sorry for her and tried—even though reluctantly— to do his best to cheer her up. He was convinced she had never wanted to admit to any sexual feelings in either herself, her husband or her son. Sexuality had to be carefully hidden from her.

Without any doubt the son had a considerable literary talent. He had already made a name for himself in his field. His teachers encouraged him in his work. It was clear that the young man's choice corresponded to his aptitudes.

Shortly after he began treatment, he fell in love with a young woman student whose radical views and frank sexual behavior fascinated him. She seduced him erotically as well as intellectually by her straightforward manners and free thinking. But soon he began to hate himself for having so helplessly been enslaved by her. He also began to understand that the young girl's freedom from tradition had a disastrous effect on her relationship with other people and on her own work. Soon she was unfaithful to him. The patient fought bitterly with himself and with her until finally he left her.

On one level the analysis revealed a narcissistic choice[18] of love object. The young woman represented his own revolt against the traditional values of his family. But on a deeper level she represented the early childhood image of his mother, which he had completely suppressed. Only now did he begin to understand how seductive his mother really had been, how her constant talk of sexual matters—clearly as a warning to him—had strengthened, and not, as he had believed, weakened the erotic bond between them.

Some time passed and the patient met another girl, quite the opposite of the former one. She was shy and inhibited and maintained strict moral standards. Very early in life she had been forced to make her own living. She had never had an opportunity to ask herself what inner resources she had, what she could expect from life and what she could offer. From the very beginning the patient felt that this girl was loyal, that he could trust her. He persuaded her to continue her studies in order to get a more satisfying job. Slowly he made her yield to his sexual wishes. He took her home to his mother, who immediately accepted her as her own child. During one session he described how the mother tried to dominate the young girl and how he helped her resist. He had also noticed his mother's open curiosity about their sex life. He was extremely proud of seeing the girl, despite her shyness, act firm with his mother, and even though they were good friends, she was never too confidential. After being engaged for a year, they got married.

Even in this satisfying new relationship the two levels of the patient's choice of love object could be easily seen. Here, too, the young girl represented himself. She—like himself—had to reorganize her life and overcome her early resignation. On a deeper level she, too, represented his mother, not the seductive one this time, but the frustrating one, as he had experienced her during latency. But the patient's attitude toward this second love object had changed entirely. He had assumed the leading role in their relationship. Motherly care and fatherly understanding had merged into an identification with an ideal parent figure. In his sex life he became the seducer and started identifying with the sexually active father.

While the first girl represented the ideal of intellectual independence and a chaotic revolt against routine and conventionality, his wife stood for moderation of judgment and for a quiet and unsophisticated acknowledgment of the facts of life. The contradictory ideals of revolt and appeasement which he encountered in the attitudes of these two women merged in time into a specific character trait of its own. Uncompromising intellectual courage fused with tender consideration for people, especially children, and for the small things in life and art.

Despite all the sadness his first love had caused him, he remembered the young woman gratefully. After all, it was she who had encouraged his break with his family's traditional way of life, and she had been the first to acknowledge him as a man and lover. I believe that we nearly always remember the transitional love objects of youth with gratitude. To the adult world they seem like earth mothers.

The establishment of a new inner balance didn't occur in spite of but rather in connection with the reactivation of the different phases in the Oedipal constellation. Both women represented a fusion of the narcissistic identification and object-directed love. But his main conflict, an ambivalent attitude toward older men, still remained partly unresolved. He constantly wavered between his longing to become a devoted disciple of a great man and his urge to compete with him and thoroughly defeat him.

When after some years the patient came back for treatment, the achievements of his youth, the transformation of his personality structure remained while his latent homosexual conflicts had caused him difficulties.

The experience of the first love of youth has a catalyzing effect on the formation of the adult personality in cases involving a fully developed Oedipus complex, relatively stable ego boundaries and a sufficient number of object-directed ego functions.

But there is also another, more tragic aspect to this experience of first love, which frequently ends with suicide. In these cases, it seems to me, the choice of the love object is either predominantly narcissistic while object-directed ego functions are poorly developed, or there is a traumatic repetition of the ego's relation to a nonloving object in early childhood. The person in the outer world to whom the emotional strivings seem to be directed lacks the dynamic quality of life and remains shadowy in outline.

If the narcissistic object choice predominates, this seems to be dangerous for the young person's already weakened sense of identity. The uncanny feeling of meeting your face in the mirror, while the world is somewhere behind it, may drive the adolescent to try to commit suicide as the only means of overcoming his fear of a complete dissolution of his personality and thus get back his integrity—at any price.

A similar catastrophic effect can be seen in cases in which the adolescent has succeeded in denying that he had been an unloved child and has consequently never learned to like anyone. The mechanism of denial often appears in the more complicated form of a manic defense,[19] which can function relatively undisturbed during latency. Later in life these young persons may choose love objects that do not requite their feelings at all. They remain neutral or may even react with hostility toward the partner's request for love. The incongruity between the insistent demands of these young people and the casual behavior of the person to whom they appeal can lead to a sudden awareness of the fact, which is otherwise denied, that they have never received any real love and, what is perhaps worse, that they themselves are desperately inhibited and unable to reach another human being. Here, too, suicide seems to offer the last chance of reestablishing the manic defense, which the ego can no longer support when confronted by a traumatic reality. Suicide is a means of rescuing the illusion of having been an extremely beloved child at the price of a complete denial of reality, of life itself.

A young man who was no longer able to support his manic defense and who was struggling with the impulse to end his life wrote to me: "My loneliness feels more as if somebody had left me than as if there had never been anybody, and it's this feeling that causes my panic."

In all these cases the first love of youth is extremely painful. It only underlines the young individual's frozen loneliness and doesn't bring about any maturation of personality. It lacks the thrill and captivation of the encounter between a forgotten world that is being revived and a new world to be discovered in the form of a beloved person.

1961

3. PSYCHOANALYSIS IN OUR TIME

Uniformity is the instrument of fear.
To acknowledge variety, complexity,
is to let experience be embraced,
integrated, and realized. This process
is the prerequisite for poetry,
practical dealings, and genuine morality.—BENGT NERMAN

Man Between Ideal and Instinct:
Sigmund Freud's Centennial in Retrospect

A HUNDRED YEARS afterward, the birth of Sigmund Freud—on May 6, 1856—was commemorated throughout the Western world. The last year of his life was spent in London, and the London County Council paid tribute to him by placing a memorial plaque in the house where he lived and which is going to be converted into a museum. The Royal Academy of Medicine and the British Psychoanalytical Society organized important commemorative festivities, international receptions and speeches as well as lectures. For two weeks the BBC scheduled daily lectures on Freud, delivered by scientists and scholars who spoke on the influence he and psychoanalysis had exerted in their respective fields.

In connection with the centennial a number of biographies of Freud were published. The most comprehensive and reliable is the one his old friend and colleague, Ernest Jones, wrote.[1] Siegfried Bernfeld's articles, published in *The American Imago,* are more sympathetic to Freud but also more limited in scope. Bernfeld died suddenly two years before the festivities and was unable to finish his work.

A flood of articles commemorating Freud appeared in journals, especially the English language ones. Perhaps the most memorable were the portrait of Freud by Alfred Kazin in *Partisan Review* and the coolly critical but nevertheless humorous account of Freud's mother in *Commentary,* by his niece, Judith Bernays Heller. Among the critical evaluations, the writings I attached special importance to were Manes Sperber's study in *Encounter,* which was a reminder of the fact that the Adlerian school was still alive, and a piece by the theologian Hjalmar Sundén, who with a great deal of empathy analyzed the relation of psychoanalysis and Freud to religion in *The Yearbook of Christian Humanism* for 1956.

But once you've read the biographies and the many articles concerning the man who's now turned one hundred and you've once again leafed through his collected works, it's possible that finally you will put everything aside and ask yourself thoughtfully: "Who was he really?"

Perhaps we shall have to wait another hundred years to find the answer.

His deliberate anonymity, the intense wish to subordinate himself to his self-appointed task—expressed in the analyst's practice of remaining out of the patient's sight throughout the treatment—seems to be one of the main reasons that Freud, the man, despite all that has been written about him, is so hard to understand.

On the other hand, his personality has particular qualities that are delineated more sharply than others and that must have left their mark on the psychological system he created.

Freud grew up in a liberal Jewish family and early in life was made aware of the Jewish child's special position in a Christian environment.

Because of the complex family setup, for a long time he was not quite clear as to who his father was—the old patriarch, who was the central figure in the extended family circle, or one of his stepbrothers, a large, impressive man in the prime of life.

There was one thing, however, that he never doubted; he himself was the firstborn son of a young and uncommonly beautiful mother whose love never failed him and who gave him the sense of inner triumph that later helped him to resist long, stormy opposition.

When he was young he underwent a decisive personality change. His longing for external power and the material comforts of life gave way to the idealist's somewhat ascetic outlook on the world accompanied by strict discipline in his work and a total lack of concern for material success. Characteristic, finally, of Freud's personality was the diversity of his intense interests, which included scientific experiments, historical research, philosophical speculations as well as formulation of a synthesis of art.

Respectfully, but decisively, Freud dissociated himself from the Mosaic faith. Nevertheless, he was very firmly anchored in Jewish history and tradition. I should think that the discovery in psychoanalysis of the emotional significance of language and its importance in shaping consciousness has to be seen in the context of a striking feature in Jewish history, namely, the special position of the linguistic tradition. The word shapes consciousness and not the other way around, said Freud. Only when we have named something do we separate it from the background and can we then start incorporating it into our world of perceptions. He refrained from using any instruments in his treatment because he thought that the psychotherapeutic result depended exclusively on the verbal relationship between patient and analyst.

Freud was often enough forced to defend himself against those who claimed that the sick cannot be helped by mere talk, and he would exclaim:

> By words one of us can give to another the greatest happiness or bring about utter despair; by words the teacher imparts his knowledge to the student; by words the orator sweeps his audience with him and determines its judgment and decisions. Words call forth emotions and are universally the means by which we influence our fellow-creatures. Therefore let us not despise the use of words in psychotherapy.[2]

Freud came to the conclusion that it was words that sustained tradition. In the same way that Rousseau considered man's prehistory to be a mirror of the childhood of humanity, Freud pointed out that childhood is the individual's prehistoric age. The history of an individual is expressed in words during analysis just as the early history of mankind has been described in religious writings. He believed that the history both of the individual and of mankind could be interpreted and that by patiently adhering to the word you could find out "what really had happened"—the truth.

The respect for the verbal tradition which is particularly characteristic of the Jews must be related to their totally abstract concept of God, which does not include any concrete symbols. Moreover, the power of the word has been especially evident to a people that has been able to exist for two thousand years as a spiritual but not a geographic entity. This is why the word became their homeland and their soil.

The question of religion preoccupied Freud throughout his life, but he never found a comprehensive solution. It is often said that he dismissed religion by referring to it as a mere general neurotic obsession. When we think of the innumerable rituals of the Mosaic religion, we cannot deny that the claim is somewhat justified. But on one occasion he wrote to Oskar Pfister, a priest and one of his earliest students, that "the beauty of religion certainly does not belong in the domain of psychoanalysis."[3] This was a most ambiguous statement, which also implied that he was aware of the aesthetic and artistic elements in religion. Toward the end of his life he assumed a more positive attitude. He thought that the power of religion lay in the new response on a broader, collective basis to an earlier, archaic object relationship. The powerful father figure of childhood appears once more when an adult in trouble seeks comfort in God the Father's overwhelming omnipotence, knowledge and justice.

Freud's shifting attitude toward religion has not had a favorable influence on the later contribution of psychoanalysis to the psychology of religion. Freud's followers adopted his ambivalence without sharing his yearning for the promised land, which is always evident in his investigations into the psychology of religion. These studies communicate to the reader something of the content of religion itself, a sense of the individual's insignificance from the point of view of eternity.

Nevertheless, it seems to me that the main thrust in psychoanalysis—of actually reliving the past as if it were a present reality—represents a grandiose sublimation of his own religious conflict, which consisted of the Jewish child's early confrontation with the Christian religion.

When Freud was barely two years old, his rival, Julius, the younger brother, who was only several months old, died. The only person who seems to have understood what feelings of anguish and guilt this provoked in him was his Catholic nannie. She took him with her to Easter services and told him that Julius, like Christ, was not really dead. He was alive in Heaven. Through the clouds he could look down at little Sigmund and rejoice at the flowers he laid on his grave.

This gentle absolution from guilt, anxiety and regret lasted only a short while. Suddenly the Catholic nannie disappeared. She had been sent to jail for theft. Shortly after this the family moved to Vienna, where Freud came under the direct influence of liberal Jewish religion and Jewish thought. He was obliged to refrain from the poetic feeling of trust his Catholic nannie had given him. Jewish children have to cope with their guilt by themselves. No father confessor will take the load off their shoulders. For Jews death is nothing but the end of life. There is no redemption of the injustice a person has suffered, nor is there any resurrection.

If we consider the differences between the sober Jewish sense of reality and the Christian hope of redemption from guilt and a life after death, we can see the psychoanalytic method as a genial compromise between the two forms of religion.

Psychoanalysis also claims that the dead are not dead. They certainly are not alive in Heaven, but they go on living inside us without our knowing it. They take part in determining our acts. They live in our conscience, in our ideals. They can possess us unto death with their hatred which turns to self-hate, or they can impel us to think and act in ways that at times make us outgrow ourselves and shatter our limitations.

During psychoanalysis the patient masters death for a short while. It is his day of judgment. But he is both the prosecutor and the prosecuted. He forgives the dead their injustices toward him and he himself is forgiven for what he has done—or failed to do. The patient makes peace with himself, with his own inner forces, just as the religious person makes peace with the power outside him, with God. This characteristic process becomes most evident in cases of depression or of melancholia. It is expressed technically in Freud's understanding that the conquest of psychic conflicts occurs by means of recollection, repetition and working through.

Psychoanalysis is related to religion and to art in its ability to resurrect the dead. Ibsen wrote that to create means to attend to your own day of judgment, and Ernst Wigforss adds in his memoirs that a person who cannot create may as well attend to his own day of judgment. In principle an artist does exactly the same as an ordinary patient in psychoanalysis; he re-creates the past so that it becomes a living reality. That is why fairy tales so often begin with the naïve, anticipatory words "Once upon a time . . ." and end with the somewhat diplomatic assurance ". . . and they lived happily ever after."

In *Zueignung* Goethe conjures up the past and invites his reader to forget the present together with him and turn his gaze on the past.

> *Was ich besitze seh ich wie von weitem*
> *und was verschwand wird mir zur Wirklichkeit.*

("What I own I see receding/And reality becomes the thing that disappeared from me!")

The climax of psychoanalytic treatment occurs when reality is experienced as dreamlike and the past as something real and tangible. At that point we can no longer discern any differentiating line between analytic technique and artistic creativity.

Two other features in Freud's personality—his interest in historical research and in scientific investigation—have helped place depth psychology on the borderline between science and the humanities.

It should not be too difficult to discover the reasons for this double orientation apparent first in Freud and later in psycho-analysis.

Who would become a historian if not a child who from his most tender age repeats over and over again the same question that the chorus in antiquity asked a grown-up man in the same condition: "Who gave you life?" And what child who felt safe in his mother's immense love would not with respectful admiration try to explore the immutable laws of nature?

I think we can say, in short, that Freud's problematic rela-tionship with his father made him a historian whereas his relationship with his mother determined his interest in science.

The most remarkable characteristic in the practice of psycho-analysis—namely, the use of scientific methods to explore psychic phenomena—has often been discussed. But Freud's scientific approach has also had other effects on the theory of psychoanalysis. It is manifest in the alert passivity that defines the analyst's relationship to the patient. He is willing to wait until the patient himself hits upon a solution. Freud believed that in psychoanalysis there was no need for a specific process of synthesis; the individual person could handle it much better than the analyst.

Where does Freud get this optimism which his patience is grounded in? From his belief that nature heals. The role of the therapist is restricted to removing obstacles that stand in the way of this process. "Psychoanalysis cannot do anything that under favorable conditions would not happen of its own accord," he once said. And when he looked back at a treatment that had been terminated long ago, he added thoughtfully that the story of the patient's recovery was no less interesting than the story of how he became ill.

Freud had the same confident and optimistic attitude toward all maturation processes and warned against pedagogy that was all too active.

Man's problem, however, lies in the fact that he does not want to surrender passively to the laws of nature. He also wants to interfere and change their direction. Freud himself understood this very clearly:

> Everyone who has begun to divine the magnificence of the world may easily lose his own tiny ego. Immersed in admiration and humility, he easily forgets that he himself is part of these forces and that he should try, according to his ability, to affect the course of events in this world, where the most insignificant is no less wondrous and meaningful than the greatest.

But this also presents the dilemma of psychoanalysis. Bound to an imperturbable and consistent determinism, it must at the same time acknowledge the unfailing impulse in man to rebel against the laws of nature.

Occasionally there is a tendency in psychoanalysis to forget the human purpose of life. It is reluctant to deal with the question of where a person is heading and what meaning he will give to his life. The neglect of teleology in the interest of a somewhat one-sided historical determinism may easily lead to the conclusion—within the psychoanalytic way of thinking— that man has a past and a present but stands facing the future empty-handed.

This inner discrepancy is even more pronounced when we consider that Freud devoted his whole life to dispelling the impediments of magic and elucidating the biological and cultural boundaries of necessity in order to achieve a definite goal, namely, to expand and stabilize human freedom.

The problem I have indicated has probably more of a theoretical meaning than a practical one. The British analyst Joan

Rivière, one of Freud's own students, has given a good example of this. She describes Freud as a man who sought the truth—"but for reasons that were outside his own self." He realized this, too, but did not draw any theoretical conclusions from the insight. His life itself stands as a brilliant example of sacrifice to a cause he thought was worth living for.

Freud experienced the dualism between his interests in history and in the natural sciences with a special intensity. He was willing to accept the fact that man is ruled by natural laws; however, he knew, too, that man creates his own history. Freud the historian discovered the opponent of nature. Tradition, in both a collective and an individual sense, plays against the instincts. The will to achieve order and to dominate rises up against the chaos of the elements. In the midst of these powerful forces we find the ego driven forward irresistibly by the blind demands of its craving but at the same time restrained and tied down by orders and restrictions that people have imposed on themselves through a long period of evolution. One has to agree with Freud when he becomes the spokesman for the repressed ego, which sometimes feels life is not all that easy.

The function of the ego as an intermediary between these two tendencies represents the human condition, because that which is essentially human has always occupied the unique position between spirit and nature.

The idea that spirit and nature can be united harmoniously in the personality represents a vital advance in the struggle for tolerance. It frees people from a sense of anxiety and horror at natural and spontaneous manifestations of life because the conscience no longer condemns these as evil and dangerous.

It has been pointed out many times that Freud was influenced by Goethe, who—inspired by antiquity—had a similarly peaceful view of man. But it seems that the longing to be able to unite spirit and nature, instinct and idea has always been present in some form or another in man. Pascal believed that nature had to be disciplined and that the spirit was help-

less without the mercy of God, and yet he was vaguely aware
that people could not do without either of them:

> *Il ne faut pas que l'homme croît qu'il est égal aux bêtes ni aux*
> *anges, ni qu'il ignore l'un et l'autre, mais qu'il sache l'un et l'autre.*
> [Man should not think that he resembles animals or angels, nor
> should he ignore either of them, but he must be familiar with both.]

Freud is the first person to apply the thoughts and hopes of
philosophers to a practically useful system of modern psychology.

Probably the development of Freud's own personality provided the basis for his concept of the anatomy of the psychic
personality.

When he was a mature man, Freud was surprising in his
proud solitude, his generosity and his tolerance. He developed
a psychological method which would help people overcome
unconscious psychic conflicts, but he was far from positing an
absolute formula for psychic normality. He had too much respect for illness and the positive forces that are tied to it.

"A man should not strive to eliminate his complexes," he
wrote to his colleague and friend Sandor Ferenczi, whose life
was a constant worry, "but to get in accord with them: they
are legitimately what directs his conduct in the world."[4] During
the period of political liberalism it seemed very clear to him that
every person had to discover for himself how much he wanted to
diverge from the average. Freud himself took very little advantage of freedom. "I support an immeasurably freer sexuality
although I have availed myself but little of it,"[5] he wrote to
a friend.

If the succeeding generations of psychoanalysts inherited
anything from him besides a new science, the first real psychology that had freed itself of physiological hypotheses,
then it is a penetrating admonition to think independently and
to have the courage to defend one's opinions. In a letter to
Pfister he wrote: "The value of what we write must be in the
fact that it does not contain anything that can be accepted on

the basis of authority alone but everything that is in it can be presented as a result of one's own assiduous work."

Freud's demands for intellectual independence and freedom in thought and science show how he developed from a Jewish child in Vienna to a European who was securely anchored in Western culture and tradition. When he quotes a diary entry by Leonardo da Vinci, it sounds very much like what he wrote to Pfister:

> *Wer im Streite der Meinungen sich auf die Authorität beruft, der arbeitet mit seinem Gedächtnis anstatt mit seinem Verstand.* [He who during an exchange of opinions refers to authorities works with his memory, not his brain.]

The uncompromising nature of Freud's occasionally heroic attitude, his moral strength and his intellectual independence were the barriers that he erected against his own passionate, impetuous and fundamentally tyrannical character, which, in addition, contained strong passive tendencies. Once in a while these would drive him to be uncritically dependent, for a short time, on people who could not live up to his expectations.

His obviously demanding impatience, the impulse to cut the Gordian knot with one stroke, developed slowly during his youth into the observer's alert but patient attitude. However, the twenty-eight-year-old man could still complain to his fiancée that there "was something wild within him, which as yet had not found any proper expression."[6]

When we look back on Freud's scientific output we can see how his own struggle for self-control led, toward the end of his life, to a distinct confession of spiritual immortality.

The last work Freud completed was *Der Mann Moses und die monotheistische Religion* (*Moses and Monotheism*). It was written after 1933 and contained a timely theme: Freud asked, "Who is a great man?" He gave different answers but found no final solution. But the essence of his thought is that a truly great man is not dependent on his origins. He need not call upon his inborn ties with race, kin or nation. His strength lies in his spiritual power and inner conviction. Finally, the spiritual bond with people could prove to be stronger than the natural ties. Moses, Freud wrote, was not a Jew but judging by the evidence, an Egyptian. He abandoned his own people and chose the Jews to carry his monotheistic faith. By means of a decision made by a foreigner, the Jews not only received their religion but also in the course of time acquired permanent character traits.

Moses and Monotheism is probably the only text by Freud that pertains clearly to present-day politics. But the figure of Moses had always fascinated him. In his everyday life Freud identified with Joseph, the youngest, and at times he also provided for no less than 20 members of the family. But in the realm of science he was Moses the lawgiver on his way to a new and unknown land, surrounded by people who were not always faithful to him. At a time when his break with Jung weighed heavily upon him, Freud anonymously published in 1914 a work of indisputable autobiographical nature: *Der Moses des Michel Angelo* (The Moses of Michelangelo).

Freud claims that when Michelangelo created the statue (which today is in the Church of San Pietro in Vincoli in Rome), he did not adhere to the historical model. The Biblical Moses was a violent man. When he saw the deceit and faithlessness of the barbarians, he was overcome by a feeling of hatred and contempt for this primitive horde of shepherds. In a blind rage he destroyed his own work and broke the tablets of law.

But in the Moses that Michelangelo depicted the emotional storm had already calmed down. This Moses would not destroy his work. At the last moment he saved the tablets that were about to slip from his fingers. He had himself under control. He had mastered his task:

> The giant frame with its tremendous physical power becomes only a concrete expression of the highest mental achievement that is possible in man, that of struggling successfully against an inward passion for the sake of a cause to which he has devoted himself.[7]

The artistic effect of this statue is due to the tension between the inner fire and the external calm of the pose. Here also lies the secretive attraction of Freud's own personality.

The components of Freud's own conflict were of a general human character—as I have pointed out—and they formed the foundation of his ideas on the dynamics of the psychic personality. But the solution, the distribution of emphasis in such a power game, varies from individual to individual. Freud gave only an example, and a very exceptional one at that, of a possible answer, yet he himself warned against considering himself a model. No psychoanalyst can know beforehand how the patient's inner balance will be affected during treatment. Here, as elsewhere in psychoanalysis, the patient has the last word.

1956

Psychoanalysis and Morality

I have one passion only, for light,
in the name of humanity which has
borne so much and has a right to
happiness.
—ÉMILE ZOLA, *J'accuse* (1898)

Finally we should not forget that the
analytic relationship is based on a love
of truth (that is, on the recognition
of reality), and excludes every form of
pretense and deceit.
—SIGMUND FREUD, *Selbstdarstellung*
(1910)

THE TRUTH

SIMPLE FACTS and unequivocal causal relationships
have a tendency to fade into the background when the
first heat of battle has subsided. They lose their topical aspect.
Now that psychoanalysis has reached a stage of relative con-
solidation, it is easy to forget some of its basic assumptions. The
psychoanalytic method can thus be reduced to a form of treat-

ment upon which its meaningful historical origins have only a latent, or indirect, influence.

Today everyone believes he knows that Freud was against "morality" and that psychoanalysis excludes all ethical valuation. People seem to have accepted it as a treatment which will "liberate your instincts" and curb your "inhibitions." It may not, however, be equally acceptable to bring up the consequences and responsibilities this freedom entails. The analyst, as everyone knows, is not to have any goals. The patient should not be influenced in any way.

We agree with those who work enthusiastically to keep psychoanalysis free of values and standards, but we add carefully that they may have made it a bit too easy on themselves. Should there not be more aspects to a treatment of the total personality that is as far-reaching and as protracted as psychoanalysis is? Why dwell on just one aspect?

Perhaps the time has come to review the assumptions on which Freud worked when he created the psychoanalytic method, and his own moral stand, which he shared with the radical élite of his time in the fields of science, art and politics.

When Freud set out to examine the nervous complaints of his patients, he did so with the same passion for truth that he had applied earlier while studying protozoa under the microscope. He realized that the material under observation could not be perceived such as it was, if from the beginning one assumed an emotional attitude that limited or even anticipated the observations. If psychic phenomena are classified in terms of set reaction patterns, such as sick-healthy, repulsive-attractive, useful-superfluous, etc., the observer has already assumed a fixed point of view which forces his examinations into predetermined channels. Therefore Freud turned away from his own set of values for the sake of one single principle: acknowledgment of the truth, which for him meant first of all an acknowledgment of causality. The need to find the truth was the absolute moral force that drove him to discover the laws governing the psychic processes. The psychoanalyst's so-called lack of values is nothing other than a conscious disconnection of emotional and moral reactions during the time the work is in process. "It doesn't befit a doctor to make emotionally toned reproaches," Freud once said. Nor to show too vivid an optimism, we might add.

From the standpoint of truth, daily occurrences in human life took on changed proportions. Small matters became meaningful—and the important things became less impressive. Freud noticed early that the loud-voiced expression was not always the meaningful one. He also saw that all of us would like to believe that those things we dislike are also things that are wrong.

The conscious and temporary disconnection of affective and moral reactions is an essential prerequisite for psychoanalytic treatment. This state lasts only as long as the work is underway and in no way represents the psychoanalyst's outlook on life. Freud had a great deal of respect for morality's regulating barriers in human society. Prejudices also had to be dealt with carefully. "They are powerful things, deposits of useful, indeed, even necessary stages of development in the history of mankind. They are retained by affective forces and the war against them is hard to wage."

Freud undoubtedly had a strong personal motive for his life-long, obstinate insistence on the truth. Moreover, he was also a brilliant exponent of the search for objective knowledge—unobscured by emotions or by social and ethical norms—characteristic of his age.

In a lecture on Freud and his times the Swedish critic Gunnar Brandell once discussed the way in which science and art—especially in France—were united in a quest for objectivity and open-mindedness. The Swedish writer Nils Olof Franzén's study[1] of the literary manifesto and moral stand of Émile Zola reveals a surprising similarity in the attitude both Freud and Zola had toward their work. As a result of it, they both were forced into unresolvable conflicts and perilous situations in life.

"In the end the experimental or naturalistic novel will tell the truth about people. It will do this without avoiding what is unpleasant, ugly, or repulsive. It will not moralize, but will speak of things as they are, not as they should be," Zola wrote.

When as an old man Freud looked back on his life, he said almost impatiently: "I did not seek out sexuality—it was already there, and even if it was unpleasant, I had to accept it."

You cannot tell apart the attitudes of the analyst and the author. Both demanded aloofness, neutrality and objectivity.

"He must adhere to observed facts, to a scrupulous study of nature, if he doesn't want to become entangled in false conclusions. He consequently disappears, he keeps his feelings to himself, he presents only what he has seen." This is Zola's advice to his colleagues. The psychoanalyst sits, as everyone knows, behind the patient in a state of relaxed *gleichschwebender Aufmerksamkeit* (evenly posed attention). He is invisible.

It was not only his quest for an objective description of human phenomena that aligned Freud with the pioneers of his times, such as the physiologist Bernard, the neurologist Jean Martin Charcot, or the writers Zola and Balzac. He also shared their conflicts, which by the law of nature inevitably resulted in a tense relationship between the instrument and the material. According to the physicist Schrödinger, the instrument determines not only what we discover but also the way in which we perceive this discovery. When man himself becomes an instrument for recording the relationship between people, this conflict is dramatically accentuated.

Franzén has described in an utterly fascinating way this insoluable inner antagonism in Zola's life and work: "A work of art is reality viewed through a temperament," said the man who demanded that the public never hear the author cry or laugh at his characters.

The tension between a person's subjective reaction and objective recording has stimulated the development of psychoanalytic theory. Sometimes objectivity has been accentuated, at other times the inevitable element of the psychoanalyst's own subjectivity. But there has always been an awareness that both exist. The patient is also a work of art, whose emotional development evokes changes in the feelings of the analyst. This forms the subdued backdrop which the patient's emotions strike in resonance. If the music is reflected off a wall, the harmony is extinguished. The distinct tones are heard; however, they have lost their meaning.

The demands Freud makes in his attitude toward the patient are conflicting ones. He maintains that the analyst's personal detachment be a prerequisite to an objective interpretation of phenomena. Nevertheless, in one of his classical case histories he says that "loving absorption" is better than "condescending arrogance" if one wishes to understand the patient's difficulties. It is demanded that the psychoanalyst have a firm sense of values and that he behave with more propriety than ordinary people, because in certain situations he has to function as both a teacher and a role model. In a letter to Jung he goes even further and points out that a positive transference is necessary if the patient is to get well: "If it is lacking, the patient doesn't want to make an effort or doesn't listen when we translate his material for him. It is essentially a cure through love."[2]

The discrepancy between the wish to achieve the maximum objectivity and impassioned, strictly disciplined temperament was not an obstacle, but on the contrary a productive force in the life work of both Freud and Zola.

Who reads Zola today? Very few people. Who remembers that he wrote the first proletarian novel? Perhaps a few more. But anyone the least bit educated is familiar with the role Zola played in the Dreyfus trial. The echoes of his writings in defense of an innocent accused man resounded far beyond the French border. Zola achieved immortality as a result of his moral stand. He became the conscience of Europe. The man who wanted only to describe his times objectively and without emotional involvement became the spokesman of the oppressed, the depraved, the ugly, the poor and the insignificant. Even they, as Franzén says, can "play a part in a tragedy that to us is as moving and rousing as the great luminary characters of classical tragedy."

Freud was an enthusiastic admirer of Zola. In 1900—two years before Zola's death—he gave a lecture on his latest book at the B'nai B'rith lodge.

This course of development appears even more striking in modern painting—especially in France. Modern artists began by objectively studying the external shifting play of light by means of scientific methods. But light falls on people as well. Beauty steps down from its marble pedestal and joins the bourgeoisie in their picnic on the grass one bright summer day. The common man steps out in all his ugliness; the washerwomen with their muscular arms, the emaciated ballet dancers showing their scraggly knees and distorted torsos. Huge peasants with the signs of poverty and apathy in body and soul eat potatoes today, tomorrow and every day of their life, without any hope of change. The light penetrates farther, corroding mystique and halos. The clown is no longer a magician, he is now a helplessly lonely social outcast. Mary Magdalene, the innocent sinner, becomes an aging, hungover prostitute. Her face tells us of an almost repulsive lack of illusions. In the Nordic countries Christian Krogh showed with words and imagery how Albertine, the innocent peasant girl from the country, was crushed by the cynical debasement of love among the middle class, the schism between sexuality and tenderness prevailing at that time and against which Freud struggled all his life.

Like many writers and painters, the founder of modern psychology has described the human condition, without embellishment or wishful thinking. If anyone has shown the scars that "the fight for survival" leaves on every person's face, it is he.

The objective, scientific study of human behavior led to the rehabilitation of the mentally suffering human being. Freud understood the heavy burden of bitter self-contempt borne by the sexual deviate, the neurotic's hopeless struggle with the uncontrollable conflicts within him, the insane person's fear of spiritual death and his groping for a reality that to him seems remote and alien. He showed that seemingly unmotivated anxieties and bad habits in children were well rooted in the course of thought and mode of experience which corresponded to their era. The sweet dolls and little cherubs that everybody liked to see around them vanished from the fantasy world of adults— more or less forever. He knew that a child could experience the feeling of love with an unreserved passion that he would never be capable of producing as a grown-up. With Freud the child became a human being from the start, from the day of his birth.

Freud never said it in so many words, but in all his writings, and not least in the case histories, we can sense his respect for the suffering human being. He never limits himself to describing only the symptoms of the patients, but brings up also their healthy qualities, their intelligence, their interests and education, as well as their kindness and charm. He never fails to note their relentless struggle against the symptom which they experience as something strange and alien. Of course, discussion of "degeneration" or of congenital diseases of the nervous system in connection with the etiology of neuroses, which flourished in Freud's time, has since disappeared.

When time and time again he pointed out that the patient has a right to be sick and that no one can be forced to be healthy, he formulated a sound principle of psychotherapy that expressed the sense of tolerance that we can scarcely surpass in our time.

Zola, Freud and many other prominent figures of the period helped put an end to the arrogant shoulder shrugging with which the so-called insignificant people were dismissed. They are insignificant only because of our indifference, our prejudices and our insecurity.

Freud proved that once in his life every person lives the tragedy which acquired words and form in the struggle of a lone Greek king against blind faith. The universal human drama, which pronounces us guilty in spite of knowing better, was revealed by means of a method founded on the love of truth and the temporary exclusion of the observer's private moral and emotional reactions.

Today when someone accuses Freud of digging into so many disgusting and (fortunately) well-hidden nooks of our soul—a thing for which Zola and Balzac, among others, are also reproached—we can in calm retrospect reply with what has been said of Balzac: *"C'est de la nuit, qu'il a fait le jour"* ("From the night he created the day"). Sometimes when a patient asked Freud what use all these detailed memories would be to him, he answered calmly: "Only a good-for-nothing is not interested in his past."[3]

As a matter of fact Freud could have remained a private scholar in Vienna who occasionally published some curious clinical observations and spent his days in peace and quiet—at any rate until 1938. Psychoanalysis has become so overwhelmingly influential in our own time only because it was created by a man who treated the occasionally contradictory results he came across as spontaneous and consistent insights. In the love of truth, the search for objective knowledge and emotional certitude made a durable alloy which protected the newly acquired knowledge against the opposition it naturally has had to face. During a period of particularly great hardships he wrote to Sandor Ferenczi:

> It is very possible that this time we will truly be buried as a funeral dirge has so many times been sung for us in vain. This will bring about a great change in our personal destiny but not in science. I am as certain of this as I was fifteen years ago.[4]

Like so many other American poets, Randall Jarrell is also a prominent critic of culture, with a feeling for the cultural aspects of psychoanalysis. He thinks that Freud, in the same way as other great men in the Western world, believed in achieving freedom through truth:

> If we know the truth, the truth will set us free—those differing and contradictory truths that seem, nevertheless, to the mind that contains them, in some sense like a single truth? And all these things, by their very nature, demand to be shared.[5]

Freud was able to fulfill through the psychotherapeutic principles his wish to share with others what he had understood. His point of departure was the self-evident fact that the patients were no less intelligent than he. They were capable of sharing his knowledge and using his method to understand the internal and external circumstances that had determined their development. Certainly at times he was ambivalent about the possibility of man's acquiring greater inner freedom and truth. Despite his pessimism, he was convinced throughout his life that perceiving the truth—how it really had come to be—protects us against mental illness and that an ordinary person can very well acquire this insight. Truths that are given to patients from the outside lack the unique quality of intuitive certainty that accompanies the ongoing process of inner restructuring. They become nice gifts that you put in a showcase to view on Sundays. Unfortunately, they are not of any real use in daily life.

Sometimes we have a disheartening feeling that many people nowadays are getting tired of this demand for activity and independence. It is too hard. Is the vision of the Renaissance and the Age of Enlightenment approaching its end? The historian T. Lindbom seems to think so, and so does the author Arthur Koestler in affirming a similar development. But the psychoanalyst Erik H. Erikson reminds us that these ideals form an integrating element in our demand for personal freedom and integrity. The individual's independence to evaluate and to act is a precondition of public justice.

Certain new tendencies of development in the psychotherapeutic trends that emerged after the Second World War have strengthened our misgivings. The memories of barbed wire and gas chambers cast their shadows upon the survivors. The evil that we thought we could dismiss as superstition and nightmare is a present threat everywhere. The force of destruction, stripped of ornamental ideologies, is in our midst. Well-meaning people from all walks of life are joining forces to save the individuals who—so we think—are floating around in modern mass society without any foothold, belief or lodestar.

In such an age it is easy to forget the healing powers of nature that are concealed within man. The psychotherapist loses his patience and calls for help from the outside. Appeals are made to church, state and science, as well as to priests and philosophers. It is impossible any longer to close our eyes to the fact that our contemporaries have a greater need for a new orientation to existence, but they no longer believe that they by themselves are able to discover new ways of life.

For Victor Frankl, the Austrian psychiatrist, who experienced the Nazi hell from the inside, the concept "psychic health" is synonymous with "a meaningful life."

> The first and most important goal of mental health should be to stimulate man's desire for meaning and offer him concrete possibilities to find a purpose. Because to direct your life toward a goal is of central importance. There is surely nothing in the world, I venture to say, that would so effectively help one to survive even the worst conditions, as the knowledge that there is a meaning to one's life.[6]

During a discussion concerning the most convenient time for terminating psychoanalysis, one of the participants, Dr. René de Monchy, said: "Analysis can be terminated when the patient feels that the life he is leading at the moment somehow corresponds to what he has wanted it to be."

The similarity of the statements is undeniable. But there is also a pronounced difference in tone, in the very style. Frankl is making an appeal to the therapist to open a new and meaningful world to the person who seeks his help. The other has a vigilant attitude. He lets the significance grow from within the patient himself, without drawing up either rules or guidelines.

The existential psychologists believe that in order to get well a person has to make his choice from among the existing ways of life. He has to learn to say yes or no. But all the while his inner significance is determined by the outside, so to speak, or by religion, it is like a gift from his own age. Only then can he overcome the sense of meaninglessness which is the basic human emotion he encounters the moment he steps into the world.

For a psychoanalyst it is difficult to accept meaninglessness as the fundamental point of departure for human development. We prefer to see it as a psychopathological phenomenon, a feeling of alienation toward oneself and the world, based on unconscious conflicts in object relationships. Or we can see it simply as an expression of inadequate knowledge. Persistent study may sometimes be the best remedy for it.

Freud considered psychic phenomena as being part of the

general biological process and as such meaningful manifestations of organic life. He proceeded from the premise that every human expression of life is *a priori* meaningful. His contribution was to show that as a matter of fact the apparently meaningless is a human way of expressing a completely understandable and acceptable content. The paralyzed arm of a hysteric may imply a genuine human conflict between a natural attachment to an admired father and the conscience which repudiates this feeling.

Anna O., whose real name was Bertha Pappenheim, was twenty-one years old when she began to be treated by Breuer and Freud. She offers an exceptionally fine example of how the dissolution of a neurotic symptom may in time lead to a totally astonishing release of energy even if the basic conflict remains partially unsolved. Bertha Pappenheim never married. She became an active feminist and had a somewhat ambivalent relation to men. But after the treatment, the spoiled upper-class girl who was used to luxury and leisure developed an intense urge to help people in need. She started out modestly as the supervisor of a children's home and in time became Germany's first social worker and the founder of several institutions for training and education in "Soziale Frauenarbeit" (Women's Social Work). Her sphere of activities became all the more extensive and she undertook expeditions of aid to Roumania, Poland and Russia to rescue children whose parents had perished in pogroms.

Could any therapist who was called in to see the young lady in a villa outside Vienna, where she spent her time in voluntary confinement with her mother, have imagined or even suggested such a career? Not only the patient but also the therapist must bow in amazement when the surprising moment in all human development occurs. And why not admit to this limit?

Now the objection may be raised that Bertha Pappenheim, who was described by her contemporaries as "a noble soul in a lovely body," was an exception. We cannot expect anything similar to happen to the great number of ordinary people in need of psychic help. (It's an odd thing about "average people."

They just sit out there in the waiting room. When one steps in, he suddenly becomes something very special, a new and unusual acquaintance.) Besides, Anna O. had a secure childhood. She was protected from material deprivation and firmly anchored in her environment and tradition—indeed she remained deeply religious all her life.

Toward the end of the Second World War many psychoanalysts were seeing a completely different set of patients—people who had lived on the fringes of existence. Many of us felt bewildered by the meaningless suffering that we confronted in their fates. We grew silent, standing there with empty hands. Counseling? It seemed trivial and out of place. With a mixture of gratitude and relief we discovered that even the most disturbed ones, the people who were reduced to insanity, were able little by little, with their own strength, to give their life a new meaning. While the goal of psychoanalysis remained the same, the technique of treatment underwent significant modifications (see the last part, "Crisis of Trust and Alienation"). Our patients found their way back to daily life. The number of such seemingly "spontaneous" cases of reorientation was amazingly high among former concentration-camp prisoners.

But the treatment of these people also drew the psychoanalyst's attention once again to the life-sustaining force of sublimation—as it is popularly called—in human existence. The understanding of the importance of ideal aims and goals as a condition for mental health developed in treating severely disturbed persons. (See chapter "Reaching Safety.")

It seems to me that a mental reorientation that is firmly grounded in the individual's biological needs—and does not contradict them—is more durable because the ego ideal and aim in life have been inseparably integrated into the whole psychophysical personality. Exerting a conscious influence on the patient—however tactful, unobtrusive, even intuitively right this may be—can hardly bring out the self-evident sense of ego presence, of "reward," that a person needs in order to react spontaneously, in a free and easy manner which is also "authentic."

But once we have come that far, we have reached the boundaries of psychoanalysis. A patient who assumes new attitudes
because his instincts—the biological foundation—have under-
gone a change also becomes conscious of his own mortality. In
confronting death he gets no further than Hamlet:

> A fat king and a thin beggar are only two different kinds of dishes,
> two fares, but on the same table, that is the end of the song.[7]

Or as the nightwaiter—death—says to the guest at the hotel
for transients, which, of course, is also life itself:

> But one day it will be said of you Sir: He was.
> Of me it will always be said: He is.[8]

The perspective of eternity belongs to the dead, not to the living.

If we will not settle for this small consolation of change in
perspective, there remains only one hope: that of leaving future generations an estate of spiritual values that will continue
to live within them, in their conscience, their ideals, their goals
and dreams. Perhaps the psychoanalytic study of the functions
of conscience and of ideal formation has taken on special relevance in a period when we are only too aware how fragile our
material values are. We know far better than earlier generations how easily they can be destroyed. We can only pass on
the standards and values of Western civilization such as we
ourselves have known them and as we've set the mark of our
own generation upon them—its material values are of far lesser
account. For my part, I believe that Freud not only has been
a prominent executor of this inheritance, but, through the discovery of the unconscious, has added a new dimension to our
perception of reality, a dimension we can no longer ignore.

The awareness that we are in charge of a cultural legacy
that must undergo sweeping changes in order to remain relevant for people today is especially charged at times with conflicts of continuous change and accelerated scientific progress.
Today we are compelled to integrate a tradition that in the
widest sense of the term is humanistic and humanitarian with
the overwhelming and, for the layman, unfathomable gains in

the field of science. Perhaps we must go all the way back to the great social and ideological revolutions of the late middle ages demanding several generations of struggle before the modern era was reached, in order to sense how extensive is the task our own times confront us with; to reshape existence so that it makes room for the new without denying what has been.

People of antiquity had no such conflicts. They did not know the difference between the distant past and the present which forces the individual constantly to reconsider forms of life set by tradition. When they had to solve a problem, they took one step backward and thought they were in the remote past. "He seeks in the past a model which like a diving bell he can glide into and thus, both shielded and disguised, he can plunge into the problems of his times," writes the philosopher of religion K. Kerenyi.[9]

Here we are faced with a peculiar process: in antiquity man was obliged to give up his identity in order to attain purpose in life. Today we are accustomed to the reverse situation. We consider the future consequences of our acts, and this enhances our sense of our own identity.

In an after-dinner speech on the occasion of Freud's eightieth birthday, Thomas Mann described the way in which remnants of the ancient ego are still brought to bear upon modern man. Because they are to a great extent unconscious, they can occasionally form a sharp contrast to the need for a realistic evaluation of one's own situation.

Thus the symptom of neurosis is an unsuccessful effort to combine wishful thinking and objective reality. If the archaic mechanisms are even more deeply cut off from a form of social expression, which, of course, in a very special way the neurotic symptom still is, and have no possibility of being transposed on a socially acceptable level, they may develop a destructive force that finally makes every positive orientation toward the future impossible. Asocial conduct, pseudo-debility, personalities with a low tolerance for tension and with uncontrolled instinctive impulses testify to the inadequate possibilities for integrating the archaic instinctive impulses. The interest psychoanalysis has always shown in artistically creative people is connected closely with the fact that art—and religion—transforms these impulses to a universal human plane on which everyone can profit from them without feelings of anxiety or guilt. In their own ways both art and religion can prevent people from regressive outbursts, that is to say, from asocial behavior. Nevertheless, religion has at times also unleashed destructive forces and presented superstition and primitive magic as objective reality. Art cannot be accused of the same thing. From this point of view, we can say that in human society both psychoanalysis and art function as intermediaries in forming the synthesis between the archaic qualities and the rational parts in man himself, on the one hand, and in the environment he lives in, on the other.

When Freud used the term "Oedipus complex" to describe conflicts in people who by chance happened to call on an unknown doctor at his private practice in Vienna at the turn of the century, he bound the fate of modern man to the whole problem of guilt and penance. Totally personal conflicts became more meaningful when they could be seen from a wider perspective of human interest. Instead of being immersed in his own problems, the analysand acquires a certain distance from his troubles, a good precondition for overcoming them.

Freud has provided some examples of the way in which an active contact with the past can safeguard human dignity during a difficult period and liberate the healing forces of irony and humor. Once in 1938, during a conversation with Theodore Reik concerning racial prejudice, he said in passing:

> Look how impoverished the poet's imagination really is. Shakespeare, in *A Midsummer's Night's Dream,* has a woman fall in love with a donkey. The audience wonders at that, and now, think of it, that a nation of sixty-five millions have . . ." He completed the sentence with a wave of his hand.[10]

Freud never condescended to mentioning Hitler's name. Apparently he did not want to contribute to making him immortal.

Francis Bull, professor of literary history at the University of Oslo, has always been a respected teacher. But in the concentration camp at Grini, the prisoner F. B. was hardly aware that, with his lectures to his fellow prisoners, he became the first group therapist in Norway. Over and over again he reminded the others that it was not the first time Norway had been hit hard by hard times.

By establishing a connection backward in time, he made the existence of his fellow prisoners into a meaningful link in the age-old struggle for the freedom of Norway. His lecture "Then and Now" begins like this: "Not only in 1940 but four hundred years ago as well—in 1537—our country was invaded by foreign soldiers."[11] This factual historical information must have sounded comforting under conditions where books were banned and time seemed to stand still. Absalom Pederssön, a priest who lived in those times, did not like the fact that the German Hanseatic merchants dominated Bergen, the largest city in the country. "They have settled down here and are acting as if this were their home," he said. The lecturer may have had a little glint in his eye when he repeated the priest's description of the experiences of one Norseman who had sailed to Danzig, where he was greatly angered by the lack of German hospitality. When his German hostess demanded that he pay for his beer and food, he was insulted and exclaimed that in Norway it wasn't customary to pay for hospitality. But the woman said that it was in her country.

And the lecturer ended his account by saying that everyone who today had experienced German hospitality would do what the unknown Norseman in Absalom Pederssön's story did when he finally came home, "fall on his knees and kiss the holy ground he was about to set foot on."

Freud believed that a humorous effect is sometimes achieved by the displacement of a small detail. This relatively harmless anecdote from the middle of the sixteenth century, describing the anger German stinginess provoked in an unknown Norse traveler, created a distance to the dangers and the uncertainty that surrounded the prisoners and the entire nation.

His feelings for his own country avoid the well-known mixture of pride, sentimentality and vengeance. We are presented with a genre painting instead of a chauvinistic picture of a battlefield. His patriotism contains the intimacy and tenderness of everyday life—and a touch of humor.

One of the most common objections to psychoanalytic treatment is that the analysands become so concerned with themselves. They only worry about their own problems and turn a deaf ear when others ask for help. Now we can say that no one is more self-involved than a person who struggles with conflicts that for the most part he does not understand. Neither do we take into consideration that a person with infantile fixations has a narrow horizon generally and does not have a particularly strong sense of reality. (And reality is far from being only the analysand himself and the people closest to him.) It is also made up of his place of work, his country and the culture he belongs to. When during the course of the analysis the analysand is forced to come to terms with himself and his parents, he is also forced to understand that many of their reactions which may have hurt or directly injured him were due to the environment in which they themselves grew up. Meaningless methods of upbringing become meaningful when they are seen in connection with the faith, goals and traditions of the parents. It is easier to forgive if you understand. You are forced to see that your parents could not have acted otherwise. Then you can also end the eternal inner prosecution of the powerful figures of your childhood. What has been done cannot very well be undone.

Nor can it be said that people are marked only by private conflicts within the narrow family circle. R. Löwenstein described a French patient who in analysis remembered that as a young man he had been very patriotic, something he thought he never had been. Only after that could he discover his problematic relationship with his father, who had fought on the French side in the First World War. To a certain extent ideological conflicts will always color individual human conflicts, determine their content and style, and affect their solution.

Very isolated people who suffer from feelings of alienation and unreality may sometimes experience a certain sense of relief when they start to look around at their environment and perceive that human society is not so chaotic or full of menacing dangers as they had thought. That nonetheless it is governed by certain rules and regulations. Often their path goes from books to pictures, to religion, philosophy and politics before they arrive at a sense of human community. We can understand why Erik Erikson demands that in order to practice his profession satisfactorily a psychoanalyst should have an "awareness of history." How much or how little is debatable. We must also add that there are psychoanalysts who consciously exclude all cultural and social aspects from their analytic work. It seems doubtful to me that in the long run they will be able to sustain this artificial isolation of psychopathological conflicts. On the other hand, the technique of psychoanalysis obliges every psychoanalyst without exception to be truthful and tolerant—toward the patient and toward himself. This inescapable prerequisite for psychoanalytic treatment contains both moral and cultural aspects.

1962

Have Neuroses Increased?

TWO ARGUMENTS emerge, like a continuous thread, in the general discussion concerning questions of social psychology and mental health: Neuroses have increased in our time and something has gone wrong with the society we live in. Belief in progress, the will to fight, the pleasure in the achievements of social reform and the greater security are all disregarded. A gray veil of unrest and perplexity has settled over what was healthy, new and confident. Even politically radical and active people are affected by inner doubts as to whether it was worth it to go on fighting for social progress. Hasn't the increase in neuroses shown that the improvement in the material living standard doesn't make people any happier? On the contrary, they seem to grow only more dissatisfied. Bodil Koch, the former minister of the Department of Education, expressed this point of view last year (1956) at a conference of homemakers in Copenhagen under the auspices of the Nordic Association: "We should be clear about it; behind the conventional facade of the welfare state, people are often sad, depressed, and lonely. It may sound shockingly reactionary, but the fact is that there is a close connection between toil and human well-being."

Erich Fromm,[1] among others, expresses himself even more

categorically: society—that is, democratic society—is sick. The individual is forced to be maladjusted because we have a pathologically distorted attitude toward what is normal. Erich Fromm is not afraid of being considered reactionary. On the contrary, he's the one who is radical. His arguments are based on extensive knowledge of sociology. His steadfast conviction of being right lends his presentation an intensity of tone that is sometimes inspiring.

In the face of such arguments we ask ourselves if perhaps we are not imperceptibly being taken in by seemingly convincing facts without making an effort to place our own and other people's misgivings in an adequate causal relationship. It may be time to examine the statement concerning the spiritual squalor of our age by simply finding out whether neuroses have actually increased, and, if this is the case, what this says about the conditions of man in our democratic society.

To begin with, it is most obvious to recall that the concept of neurosis in use today is no more than a good half century old. It stems from the discoveries of Freud. He was the first to understand that neuroses develop mainly because of psychic motives, while the somewhat older Pierre Janet still held on to the old idea that neuroses are caused by organic changes in the nervous system. This is why it is extremely dubious to talk about increase in a type of illness that has been known for only such a short time. Besides, the statistics for neuroses are extremely inadequate both in regard to number and on the basis of disparaging opinions as to what should be registered. So far it would be more correct to say that "there is a feeling" that neuroses have increased or that, with the newly acquired knowledge of the structure of psychic conflicts, we have steadily acquired a greater insight into their general scope.

Naturally the increase in the public interest in psychological questions and the unprecedented dissemination of mental hygiene has caused the concept of neurosis to lose its original meaning and become a catchall for all sorts of discomforting things.

We cannot, for example, imagine a relationship of sharper

contrast than the one between Freud's original conception of the core problem in neuroses and the wider interpretation that Fromm and his school have become spokesmen for. According to Fromm, a person is forced to reduce himself to becoming neurotic because the social institutions that he is in contact with are inimical to every natural outgrowth of life. He believes that society wishes people to be frustrated. Freud, on the contrary, starts from the premise that a person can master his conflicts by his own strength, even though he wasn't blind to the fact that there are occasionally social complications. The aim in the classical therapy of neurosis was to liberate all the potentials and make them function within the individual's actual situation. The American Gregory Zilboorg begins his book on Freud by claiming that "ever since the beginning he had considered mental health and individual freedom as nearly identical."

The psychoanalytic therapy of neurosis developed at a time when the individual had acquired an inconceivable amount of freedom in the exterior world. Man had become mobile. He could move, change his residence, choose and change his profession, find a spouse from near or far, with relative independence of social origins or religious convictions. Women had become active members of society. Children were no longer considered moody adults in miniature but were seen as developing creatures. The private individual had acquired a worldly new sense of dignity.

But man, who up to that time had lived within a narrow sphere of consciousness, couldn't benefit from the outer expansion without broadening his mental outlook at the same time. The multiplicity of the exterior world evoked the need for a greater, more sonorous echo inside man. The world outside had grown into a large, at times confusing orchestra. One was obliged to reply in polyphonic harmony. Therefore the external expansion was followed quite actively by an expansion inward. Man became a problem for himself. The unimaginable "risky enterprise inside man" was added to the risky venture in the exterior. We can understand that Erling Eng,[2] otherwise a rather critical professor of psychology, believes that what is now significant in psychoanalysis is the fact that the individual is allotted an almost unlimited amount of inner mobility, something the older concepts of human existence did not permit.

If we believe that the task of psychotherapy is to help people achieve greater freedom, mobility and psychic maturity, the question of whether neuroses have increased loses its meaning. In former times the state and the church took care of people's spiritual needs and guided them from the cradle to the grave. Now, in the welfare state, which some people seem to be able to afford to view ironically with condescension, the situation is reversed. The state takes an ever-increasing responsibility for ensuring the material welfare of people and providing them with an existence free from want. People have acquired time, surplus and, not least, the freedom to be physically mature. And as is always the case with newly acquired freedoms: there is a chaotic and perplexing period of transition. People who have lived in psychic darkness and have not assumed anything about themselves may experience an inconceivable sense of freedom that can easily turn into anxiety. But for the first time we also get a glimpse of all those dead souls who have populated the country. The purpose of mental hygiene today is to help manage the newly won psychic freedom and spiritual life. Because of this there is a fast-growing need for psychotherapy and the individual's heightened insight into erroneous and inhibited ways of development. We are faced with a phenomenon of excess energy.

In this situation it seems important not only to help people satisfy their psychic needs but—and this is equally necessary—to awaken them (this should not be confused with all possible sorts of hobbies and leisure occupations that in themselves are well meant). There are still enough oppressed and frightened people who live in a state of inner monotony without asking themselves in what direction they want to go and who accept their inner grayness and spiritual poverty because they haven't yet perceived that they have a claim to greater inner happiness. Among those who today groan over the fact that neuroses have increased so visibly, there are many who haven't understood that they themselves have helped create "neuroses" by disseminating information. How many people are there, for example, who seek help from psychotherapy or psychoanalysis after they have been in touch with the state office of sex information? People who previously felt lost and sinful have started to wonder whether their feelings of anxiety and guilt are really all that justified. They go into psychotherapy to find out if they can ease their burdens. Without intensive dissemination of information, they wouldn't have sought help but would have been resigned to live with a bad conscience, crippled emotions and diffuse anxiety. They would have hidden in their homes and wouldn't have packed the waiting rooms of psychotherapists. But neither would they then have contributed to increasing the statistics.

Perhaps the ever more widespread conception of the importance of environment for mental health has contributed to the so-called increase in neurosis. Countless people have started to doubt the idea that their depressed feeling about life and their inner paralysis really depend exclusively on their constitution or "weak nerves," factors that it is almost impossible to change. I shall give only one example that is fairly typical of the rebellion against this point of view. A young man who suffered from serious inhibition in his work had been told ever since his school days that "it ran in the family." When he began psychotherapy he said: "My parents took it for granted that you were supposed to suffer your whole life. They felt that something was wrong, but convinced themselves that it was part of their constitution. But I have had a strong sense that things could have been different. Things got jammed up someplace along the line. That's why I'm here."

Apparently neuroses will increase to the same extent that people see that "things can be different," because they will rebel against their lack of inner freedom "which has gotten jammed up." To this extent neuroses express an increased desire for freedom.

Every era seems to have its special form of anxiety. I don't know what people in the middle ages feared most. Was it to

die of hunger during the years of famine, the great burden that
their overlords imposed upon them, or the wrath of God threatening them with the eternal fires of hell? But whatever the content of their anguish might have been, there was always the
poor, helpless person's fear of being abandoned to the fickle
forces of heaven or earth. Also the neuroses that express the
special psychic conflicts of our times evolve from a core of
anxiety. But to the fear of being dependent on outside forces
is added a new one: man is asking himself more intensely than
ever if he has the time to take advantage of his own capabilities
during the brief interval which is his life, the short flash of
light in the darkness. The newly won inner freedom is accompanied by an inner concern over the question whether we
can shape our own existence, our own inner fate while being
conscious that death awaits us. Heidegger, who has called this
fear "a cultural dread," believes that it is the most developed
form of dread a person can experience. On the other hand, the
primitive dread—namely, anxiety over one's daily bread—is
experienced by everyone. Only when it has been overcome
somewhat does the concern for other people's welfare emerge,
and this he calls *"Fürsorge"* (social welfare).

The prevalence of cultural dread in our age is associated with,
among other things, the shifts in the demographic structures
such as the increased life-span and the decline in population
growth, factors that David Riesman chose as the premises for
his social and psychological analysis in *The Lonely Crowd*.

If we follow up this introduction, we can then say that the
welfare state is based on anxiety for the well-being of others,
and it gives the individual the freedom to experience his dread
of not being able to use his one and only life to the fullest
extent possible. This anguish can never be shared with others;
it is experienced individually. Neuroses, which I described as
phenomena surplus, are therefore accompanied by a specific
new form of anxiety: cultural dread.

If the anxiety for daily existence overshadows everything
else, then no cultural dread develops. People in a concentration
camp had no neuroses. While they were there, they even lost

their former neuroses. A young man who had stammered since he was four or five years old spoke quite correctly during the three years he spent in Theresienstadt. When he came to Sweden at twenty-two and started to live a normal life once again, the stammering returned, or as he expressed it, somewhat amazed, "I got back both my freedom and my stutter."

There is actually nothing new in experiencing one's own individuality as a unique phenomenon with absolute demands of development and perfection. But it used to be reserved for a small minority. It was first in democratic society that it became possible for the great majority of people to have the right and the duty to achieve inner maturity. Goethe believed that the greatest fortune of all people on earth was to have a personality, but he was surprisingly indifferent to the fact that only the sovereigns, their ministers and the *Geheimräte* (privy counselors) could permit themselves this luxury while the young sons of the peasants were captured like cattle and sold as soldiers to foreign countries. In those times this was how they balanced the ruler's state treasury.

Before the emergence of modern democracy, the great majority of people must have lived in a state of inner repression, gray inside as well as outside, and with the resigned, empty look of dead souls. As Ivar Lo-Johansson described the peasants: "The body was immediately sinful when you didn't work it for the estate," and their souls resembled "desolate flatlands where nothing but terror seemed to wish to dwell."

But the new feeling for life, with the individual himself being responsible for his psychic well-being, results not only in gains but also in losses. Much has been written about the losses—while people have kept relatively quiet as far as the gains are concerned. Let us look first at the losses.

Today we are witnessing a continuous reevaluation of human qualities. What was virtuous yesterday may no longer be quite acceptable today. Tomorrow it may be quite reprehensible. But certainly, among those who were enslaved and those materially and spiritually poor, there were certain moral qualities, and it is sad for us to see them disappear.

The short time we walk this earth, with a fleeting youth and with no defense against hunger, sickness or oppression, left us no opportunity to long for a personal delineation of the individual's existence. The collective ideals that the state and the church provided for the poor were accepted without any reflection on their content. People had to reconcile themselves to the collective dream of the poor man's happiness beyond this life on earth and as individuals they had to take pride and joy in being able to serve—the worldly lord or the spiritual one. Humble resignation and unreserved devotion, a kind of *amor fati* (love of fate), could provide a quality of simple greatness and calm to the best of the oppressed. Peace of mind, owing to the fact that one accepts his situation in the world without envy or ulterior motives, is undoubtedly more uncommon in our times, when the individual is constantly prepared to reconsider his human and social relationships. A lack of need and a sense of calm in the even rhythms of time were able to fill the surrounding world with a quiet love. Today we are pursued by a feeling that it is too late to rest, to rejoice in ourselves and in the world. The cultural dread drives us inexorably forward, toward new goals, and the happy feeling of "here and now" is overshadowed by the awareness of how short life is.

The qualities of tolerance and unpretentiousness used to be appreciated. The few moments of happiness were accepted as gifts of grace. Misfortunes were perceived as a time of visitation when a person had an opportunity to prove his enduring faith. People knew, as they did in antiquity, that "patience is the lesson of suffering." Today, in our worldly impatience, we prefer to ignore this wisdom.

But even if this silent suffering endowed certain individuals with greatness and strength, it also repressed the need to alter shameful living conditions. In his book *The Great Reconstruction*,[3] Erik Goland describes a home of abject poverty that Lubbe Nordström visited on his travels through the poor areas of Sweden. The people who lived there were "unbelievably decent, quiet, reticent, uncommunicative, uncomplaining, and remained silent most of the time." When Goland visited them

16 years later, nothing had changed. They lived in the same dilapidated house with moldy wallpaper—rats felt at home there—and the husband had consumption. Nor had their state of mind apparently changed. They seemed to be as perseverant and quiet as 16 years earlier. Is it possible there was a connection between their silent humility and the constant squalor in which they lived?

The virtues of the poor and their readiness to suffer have often blocked the fulfillment of their desire to live a decent life. The need for material improvements has seemed to them a sign of impermissible pride and self-exaltation. In its early days the labor movement was always forced to fight on two fronts, on one against the people who were actively opposed to liberation because they had the power, and on the other against those who mutely accepted bondage as an essential part of their lives. Therefore, in demanding that the rich share with the poor, the socialists were not only fighting for a new sense of solidarity, they were also struggling for the individual's right to shape his own life. They became the advocates of a new ideal of personality by helping the individual become even slightly aware of his inherent need for freedom and dignity. But it seems to me that the struggle against unnecessary and degrading suffering has created an unwarranted (and even dangerous) rejection of all suffering in general. That suffering is no longer a virtue—so be it. But if it has become unrefined (or even embarrassing), it may lead to a superficiality of life style and needless avoidance of difficulties and conflicts. And in this respect we forget that a personality is not something you get for nothing. Without conflicts, we remain diffuse, as if lacking a face.

The extent to which laymen and specialists agree in our times is touching: both believe the goal of mental hygiene is to spare people from psychic suffering. But we may wonder where actually to draw the line, if it isn't also necessary to teach a person how to deal with a conflict, to accept the consequences that may sometimes be painful, to struggle in order to find a solution or to be able to accept defeat. The image of the mature personality also includes a readiness to bear a certain amount of pain, anxiety, loneliness and misgiving without having a breakdown or feeling sorry for oneself.

It seems as if we sometimes refuse to realize that there are individuals who become neurotic because they have repressed their need to sacrifice themselves for something, no matter how much suffering it causes. I don't know how many of these cases there are. But their share in the increase of neuroses dramatically demonstrates that it is a question of surplus, a conflict with unused resources.

A child lives from day to day without a care—or at least it should—but the life of an adult becomes meaningless if he doesn't have any goals. The more mature an individual is, the more he wants to grow beyond his own sphere of interests and take other people carefully into consideration. He projects the time of completion into a remote future, beyond his own lifetime, to coming generations. Clinical experience shows that an adult can develop psychic symptoms of being poisoned if he is much too intensely concentrated on himself, and in all probability this can be applied in broader contexts as well. From a perspective that was anything but psychoanalytic, Dag Hammarskjöld observed in 1952 that "collective hysteria" and "destructive political ideals" may emerge among population groups which have no dimensions into the future or any ideological needs. A high standard of living is in itself no protection against psychic destruction. The myth of Narcissus is far from being only a poetic story about a beautiful youth who falls in love with himself. It also shows that Narcissus cannot avoid destroying himself and dying alone as a result of his all-engulfing self-love.

The need for a meaningful life is rooted deeply in man. And not only because it gives a feeling of inner continuity and relative independence from the whims of fate. But inner security is not something we get in the cradle. It is the result of an inner development which is inconceivable without a certain amount of suffering and privation. George Orwell can hardly be suspected of having denied the poor the right to a better life on earth. But the man who fought for the Spanish Republic and the poet who wrote *Homage to Catalonia* claims without the slightest sentimentality: "Most people get a fair amount of fun out of their lives, but on balance, life is suffering and only the very young or the very foolish imagine otherwise."[4]

One of the reasons why suffering has fallen into disrepute in our times is that we can no longer console ourselves by saying that some heavenly power has sent it down upon us. We've begun to understand the truth in La Rochefoucauld's words, "The whims of our nature are more peculiar than those of fate," and that to a great extent we create our own misfortunes. Furthermore, the new personality ideal demands that we fight against unnecessary suffering and overcome it. But who will decide where to draw the line between inevitability and latent change?

Evidently the direct and open confrontation with harsh reality is so frightening that it is hard for man to refrain from setting up some kind of protective medium between himself and his immediate pain. In former times suffering became the secret link between man and his God. Now it has been deprived of its metaphysical gleam. Instead, now we have a more prosaic power disturbing us in our "natural state of happiness," namely, society. Society has become a peculiar god, a *deus ex machina* in some trends of modern psychological thought. Once more the individual can throw off his responsibility for the misfortune of his life. We have not been able to utilize our own capabilities for development because "society" prevents us from realizing ourselves. We don't take exams because we aren't competitive as "society" prescribes. We become criminals because "society" has dissolved family ties. We have no morals because the value system of "society" is so contradictory. And in this way, naïve and guiltless, we explain away our share in misfortune by placing isolated sociological facts in wrong causal relationships. The individual is fixated in a childish, complaining attitude, scolding adults because they are naughty. (For surely it is adults who make up society.)

Kaj Björk wrote in *Tiden* (*Time*) (No. 2, 1956) about a neurotic dissatisfaction among people who don't want to pay high taxes but who at the same time demand that society give them all its social benefits. This can be considered a typical example of the infantile, demanding attitude of people who want society to take care of them the way their parents did when they were children, namely, without expecting any service in return.

Some of the seemingly radical psychologists, with their one-sided social criticism, have helped considerably to justify and even to encourage this point of view. Instead of viewing the dynamic interplay between the individual and the group, they see the single person helplessly wandering around in a desolate room with a closed door bearing the sign:

DO NOT ENTER!
Society

In reality, however, there have probably never been so many doors open as there are today.

People who have rashly and childishly expected social institutions to be unlimited in generosity, meeting an obligation to provide them with security, have now acquired seductive rationalizations for their irrational expectations. In this way, talented, intelligent people stagnate in querulousness and "stabilized displeasure" and add to the multitude of "neurotically discontent people." Truly, they merit a better fate. I should think that politicians have every reason to be on guard against this displeasure. The more the material needs are satisfied, the more apparent the qualities of irrational dissatisfaction become, for they can no longer be rationalized by legitimate criticism of an evidently unsatisfactory state of material things.

"Neurotically discontent people"—it would be better to call them "irrationally discontent"—blame democracy because it has made no secret of its imperfections. They demand that democracy never err, that it be absolutely good and omniscient. They don't like democracy to admit its weak points openly. A good number of the irrationally discontent people flirt with some kind of authoritarian form of government—which is very skillful in hiding its weaknesses behind an imposing facade.

But that which is absolute does not develop, nor does it offer any future perspectives. While, on the other hand, what is unfinished gives the hope that one can learn from mistakes.

"More and more I am convinced that there is no way out of chaos but to adhere to democracy irrevocably, blindly and fanatically, even to its right to get into trouble, to wage war, to make wild offensive moves, to destroy itself or its country, to oppress minorities—until it comes up with something better," the young Wigforss wrote in reference to the Bolshevik revolution in 1917. Maybe it was this illusionless but at the same time optimistic love of democracy that made him a statesman in its service.

For several years the theories of Fromm, Karen Horney and a number of others have been in the foreground of the discussion in social psychology particularly because, without knowing it, they comply with the unconscious wish a great number of people have to avoid responsibility for their own fate by putting the blame mainly on social institutions and objective, exterior reality.

Less notice has been taken of other concepts regarding the relationship between the individual and society. But then they have not furnished such neat rationalizations.

The British Institute of Human Relations, for example, represents a much more positive view of the role of the individual in democratic society. According to it, the latent meaning of the idea of democracy is a "mature" society which is well adjusted to its socially active and similarly mature members. An individual, says D. H. Winnicott, who supports this form of administration, is mature when, in relation to his age and social environment, he has reached "an appropriate degree of emotional development." We must begin with the fact that only a certain proportion of the population can reach a psychic maturity that enables people to take care of all the members of society who have not reached it, the ill and the asocial. Therefore, the psychically sound members of society are the true supporters of democracy. Through their contribution the group's inherent tendency toward social maturity is fulfilled.

If we accept this more dynamic concept of the function and significance of democracy, we can immediately understand why it seems that neuroses have increased in our times. For democracy demands psychic maturity of the greatest possible number of members, whereas other forms of government are based on the great majority's not being mature. In an authoritarian society a fear of making independent decisions and an uncritical submission to the authorities' rules and restrictions are desirable qualities. But the same features curtail the functioning of democracy and are therefore considered signs of psychic immaturity. Neuroses have increased because democracy makes greater demands on every individual citizen's sense of responsibility and independence in both word and actions.

An authoritarian constitution and a fixation on infantile attitudes among individuals result in large groups of people feeling fatalistic. On the other hand, psychic maturity implies a more optimistic basic disposition. It is possible to have experiences that in turn open up new perspectives and lead to unexpected new tasks and problems. People have accepted their role as active participants in the governing of society and not only are willing to acknowledge its authority but also will take it over within some restricted areas.

The situation of mental hygiene today would be fatefully misjudged if one were to equate psychic immaturity with neurosis. Psychic immaturity as such is a sign of inhibited development, a stationary defect. However, a neurosis is characterized as a dynamic conflict between the fully developed part of the personality and other less—i.e., infantile—impulses and attitudes. The neurotic symptom is a form of compromise in the largely unconscious struggle between different degrees of maturity within one and the same person.

The stationary group less often becomes a sustaining force

of the democratic society while with adequate help those who suffer from inhibitions in functional development can mature and become capable of contributing actively to society.

But first of all we have to make it very clear that in many cases psychic maturity is not the opposite of a neurosis. People who suffer from unconscious psychic conflicts are for the most part reliable members of society, often equipped with considerable intelligence and remarkable mental faculties. They keep their personal hell inside them secret. Their conscience, which sometimes is all too stringent, can drive them to social achievements that benefit society. Only they themselves know what it costs them. Consequently, even though Kaj Björk has grasped something essential when he talks about neurotic discontent, I believe it is more correct to speak of the irrational dissatisfaction of all those "who want to eat their cake and have it too." No doubt there are neurotics among them. But there are just as many outside this group, among people who are positive, willing to work and conscious of their responsibilities. They, too, must be allowed to have unresolved conflicts.

In other words, the task of mental hygiene today is to secure democracy by giving those who are psychically mature and those who have latent capabilities of becoming so the assistance they need in the form of counseling, psychotherapy and psychoanalysis. I think that this is where we find the striking difference between the psychotherapeutic and psychiatric methods we see today. The practicing psychoanalyst and psychotherapist will confirm the experience of Gunnar Nycander according to which "the clients that psychiatrists, and then above all forensic psychiatrists, have to consider are in most cases people who do not seek help from a psychotherapist and—when they do—they are dismissed as being unsuited to psychoanalysis or related forms of therapy."

The steadily increasing number of people who are mature enough to develop insight into their illness and are receptive to therapy may be considered a guarantee that the foundation of democracy—the psychically mature citizens—will expand and be secured. To keep the neurotics outside is not only unjust, it is also dangerous. It leads to an artificial reduction of the group that sustains democracy. This we cannot afford.

1957

POSTSCRIPT, 1967

In the field of modern social psychiatry people have also begun to realize that neurotics are not ill in social respects and should not be considered partially handicapped. In *Work and Mental Health,* a large manual published in 1969 by Tiden, its author says, "Certain features of mental illness may be consistent with extremely good adaptability to work."

A Pluralistic View of Man:
Dialogue with a Friend

> He who really wants to grasp the truth,
> that is to communicate, with him we can
> speak of anything and he can do so in
> like manner so that there is no need to be
> cautious or do harm, it is communication
> between people who are capable of change
> and prepared for it.
> —KARL JASPERS, as quoted by Tollak
> Sirnes in *Mental Health*

TOLLAK SIRNES[1] is one of the few people today who can
be called a *polyhistor,* a great and learned scholar. As
a psychiatrist and a professor of pharmacology, he is at ease in
two cultures, the humanistic and the scientific one. With a rare
intensity that occasionally borders on restlessness, he seeks
new paths, new perspectives. He is always prepared to give up
the scientific domains conquered yesterday for the possibilities
visible today and tomorrow. Perhaps he is driven on so inexorably by a desire to make up for the wasted years of his youth.
Like so many young men of his generation, he spent them in a
concentration camp instead of pursuing his studies in peace and
quiet, with his life securely ahead of him. When an avowed
humanist forms an opinion of his book, it is bound to be one-

sided. Even so, it is worthwhile having a discussion with Sirnes, the humanist, as long as we are aware that his attitude toward the problem and his methodology have been influenced by the scientist, yet remain accessible to a humanist.

Sirnes starts out by discussing the concept of "mental health," and with that he is into one of the dilemmas of psychotherapy. The concept isn't simple. Every theory of normality must be seen in relation to the patient's cultural background and also to the individual therapist's particular life experience and environment. But a therapist who doesn't know what health is or can be runs the risk of neglecting something that is essential to being ill.

The account by Sirnes is of special interest from the point of view of the present revisions in the theory of normality. It is not propitious for mental health always to adjust to the environment, as was stressed so emphatically in the past. The art of living consists of knowing when to give up and when to fight.

Adolf Meyer has made himself a spokesman for spontaneity: the individual has inherent tendencies to act spontaneously before he acquires the so-called response. Such an individual develops a natural sense of responsibility. He is aware of being the "source" of his acts and therefore capable of making a mistake. When something goes wrong people who believe that they are directed by others will excuse themselves by saying that they are victims of circumstances. Sirnes agrees with Freud that a sense of inner freedom is indispensable for mental health. Modern psychoanalytic research has again taken up the concept. Heinz Hartmann considers the relative autonomy of the ego a gauge of freedom, and it is also "a base from which freedom can be expanded." David Rapaport goes to the point when he says that "freedom lies in controlling necessity and the insight into it."[2] Maybe somewhat too ascetic a formula. There is a spontaneous experience of inner freedom when you suddenly have a new insight and the limits of your sphere of experience expand.

Sirnes mentions that the ability to be grateful is a sign of mental health, something that I believe has been forgotten in the discussion and that is directly connected with inner freedom. Gratitude is an important art. Only a person with some measure of inner freedom is able to accept generously and without reservations. Slaves are not grateful.

I don't think we can be appreciative enough of the present readjustments in the theory of normality. Individuals can no longer be considered a *tabula rasa* on which anything can be written at our discretion. The newborn child is already equipped with a certain capacity to confront an ordinary environment actively. "His majesty the baby" fascinates the adults with his charm and conspicuously permits himself to be adored by them.

As long as health was defined by a highly mechanistic psychology, we were presented with a list of splendid qualities that on the whole seemed uniformly drab and unimaginative. There may have been some people who secretly wondered whether in the end the lively unpredictability of neurosis wasn't preferable.

The most dangerous theory was the one that regarded as mentally healthy the individual who adjusted to society with the least possible friction. This had political consequences that those who promoted it could never in their gullible naïveté have imagined. The Nuremburg trials have shown how the smooth and perfect adjustment of people to an environment annihilated every individual and spontaneous form of humanity.

First and foremost I believe that it is impossible for a viable form of democracy to function if it idealizes passive acceptance or glorifies the kind of person David Riesman has described as "outer-directed." Today we are forced to live with conflicts that can only be solved in the long run. In these circumstances security is less dependent on the conflicts being solved than on the attitude prevailing while they remain unsolved, on the ability to put up with tension without becoming irritated or depressed. There is a type of mental opportunism, a tendency to be satisfied with partial solutions or false solutions, that can create *ressentiment* and contempt for the right to freedom of speech and information.

Democracy involves a sense of multiplicity and the right to the greatest possible amount of different variety. And then we must also include the extreme deviants, who are part of democracy's given "operating expenses" as Sirnes calls them. In a pluralistic society the concept of health must also be pluralistic. Of course, we may live by the reality principle. But there must also be room for the daydreamer, who isn't necessarily either neurotic or insane. Of course, we will adjust. But it is stubborn maladjustment that has made the world progress in spite of everything.

By the very fact that modern psychological research proceeds from the concept of a basic active interplay between the individual and his environment, the patient rather than the therapist becomes the one to determine what is sick and what is healthy. Ultimately it is he who decides if his existence has acquired the feeling of solid authenticity, the sign of health and freedom.

Beginning with this understanding, which I believe is mutual, I wish to discuss two problems with Tollak Sirnes, namely, his criticism of psychoanalysis and his assessment that Christianity is above all an indispensable element in mental health.

I have rarely seen any reason to start a discussion with a critic of analysis. I am not interested in recruiting converts. In therapy there are many roads leading to Rome, to the alleviation of the patient's suffering, although I believe that psychoanalysis is by far the best method for treating neuroses and neurotic personalities. At the same time the book by Sirnes was published in Norway, Martin Buber's *Sense of Guilt* became available in Swedish. Faced with Buber's irresponsible attacks on psychoanalysis, we can only meekly point out that a great prophet need not always display scientific integrity. In criticizing Freud, Tollak Sirnes follows a line of reasoning similar to Buber's. But his emotional climate is different: it is sincere and generous. Therefore it is interesting to try to answer him.

In his critique of method, Sirnes cautions psychologists against forgetting that people have a "constitutional inability to assume a scientific viewpoint" in interpreting observations and relations of cause and effect. Sirnes writes:

The fact is that by our attitude toward the patients we ourselves take part in inducing a certain experience.—No part of reality can be described except in relation to one's own or another person's point of view in a situation. Our expectations will inexorably influence what we observe and how we interpret phenomena.

I don't believe this necessary skepticism and heightened attention to the therapist's own limitations would encounter any opposition among analysts. In therapy training the would-be psychoanalyst is required to learn as much as possible to reduce his tendency to influence the patient. He must be aware of his personal characteristics and must learn to keep them at a distance, but he must also use them consciously when he thinks doing so will benefit the treatment.

Sirnes believes that the personality of the psychoanalyst plays a greater role in treatment than Freud would have wished:

> Freud recommended that the analyst "remain opaque as a mirror to the analysand and, like a mirror, show nothing but what it is shown." However, anyone who has experienced this "mirror" himself knows that in reality it remained opaque only in Freud's imagination. To his patients and students, he was on the contrary extremely transparent behind his brilliant and exceptional kindness, warmth, and authentic humanity. The demand for the analyst to remain unknown was merely a technicality, dictated by his respect for the patient's uniqueness.

Sirnes remains skeptical about Freud's idea that recovery occurs when unconscious conflicts become conscious. He is more drawn to Franz Alexander's[3] view that a new event,

> the emotional experience functioning as a corrective agent, which develops in the mutual work of the analyst and analysand, gives the patient courage to reorient himself. Because the attitude of the therapist is different from that of the authority figure in the past, he gives the patient the opportunity over and over again of confronting the emotional tensions that were unbearable in the past and of dealing with them in a different way than before.

Throughout the book Sirnes maintains a serious charge against psychoanalysis: Freud and his followers consider all feelings of guilt neurotic and believe they should be "analyzed away." He quotes the Norwegian psychiatrist Ejnar Lundebye:

Even if psychoanalysts are right in arguing that a great deal of anxiety and guilt is caused by incorrect education, we must draw the line when they start claiming that guilt is a neurosis. It is completely untenable to assert that instruction and psychoanalytic treatment can help us do away with all our guilt feelings. We must understand that there is a sense of guilt which has nothing to do with these things and cannot be removed in convalescent homes, nor by sleeping pills or psychoanalytic cures.

Nothing would be easier than to refute this accusation as completely unfounded. But then we could not reach any agreement. It is also difficult to see why this charge against this supposedly asocial foundation of analysis is so widespread, from Martin Buber to Tollak Sirnes. Perhaps a *mea culpa* may lead to better insight. Can it be that psychoanalysts themselves have unintentionally contributed to this unfortunate misunderstanding?

It is possible that the special technical and theoretical language of analysis bears a good share of the blame. A psychoanalyst is accustomed to describing the end results of treatment by dividing complicated psychic structures into their basic elements. Highly structured psychic phenomena such as the sense of guilt are not part of this essential abridgment. But this doesn't mean that the analyst isn't familiar with them. Abstract thinking in terms of models is indispensable for factual communication, but there is no doubt that it has brought about an impoverishment of style that was foreign to Freud. Modern psychoanalytic writers, such as Mitscherlich[4] and Erikson,[5] have begun to rebel against an exaggerated use of abstractions. They use everyday language more frequently, and this includes words such as "guilt," "insight" and "responsibility."

Another reason may be the special change in perspective involved in the psychoanalytic method. That which from the outside may seem like guilt, viewed from the inside turns into a pathological case. At that point the task of the analyst is not to establish the result—guilt—which in any case is apparent, but to locate the motivations in order to end the unhappy recurrences.

If at times a mother rashly hits her child on the slightest provocation, we can judge her to be guilty, and rightly so. She is not a good educator, and the child is being exposed to unnecessary suffering. If such a mother visits an analyst, he will try to ascertain her motives in order to decide whether or not she is suited for psychoanalysis. If in despair she complains that sometimes all turns black before her eyes and she is overcome by an inexplicable rage against the child, then in most cases a neurotic symptom, an unconscious emotional conflict is at work. The same mother may try to explain away her behavior in one way or another: "Sometimes I have a headache and I'm easily irritated." "My husband never uses discipline and, well, somebody has to bring up the child." This may be a sign of a relatively transparent defense mechanism working against a sense of guilt and a painful lack of inner freedom. The prognosis for this mother is good. Deep down neither of these mothers in fact wants to hit her child. But now and again a mother who doesn't show any signs of conscious or unconscious conflicts may come to see the analyst. Without a quiver in her voice she declares that she hits her children whenever it pleases her and outsiders should mind their own business. Most often she is a psychopath with a bad prognosis. Such a mother experiences no conflict and is beyond feelings of guilt. Psychopaths, says Sirnes, do not "have" any illness; that is the way they "are." Nor are psychopaths suited for psychoanalysis.

But the analyst who decides to work with the first two mothers doesn't have to remind them of their guilt. They are more aware of it than anyone else. On the other hand, if the mother admits realistically that she has harmed her child, she may free reparative forces and bring about a gradual revision of her overall educational goals and methods. To insist on her guilt would be tactless and also unwise. The Talmud says that "you cannot expect a guilty man to learn." A psychoanalyst wants his patient to redevelop and not to get caught up in anxiety and guilt.

Socially a psychoanalyst is a strictly private person. He has no rights beyond those of an individual. He is no judge in the name of law. Nor does he have the priest's authority of absolution. At best a psychoanalyst is the defense attorney of an oppressed person. But the psychoanalytic defense attorney soon makes a remarkable discovery: there are patients who don't want to be acquitted. Guilt is like a junction in the development of their personality where the essential characteristics, the formation of ideals and the specific patterns of behavior merge. Liberation from such a sense of guilt is experienced as a threat to one's personal integrity because it would break down highly integrated ego functions.

Perhaps the analyst's attitude toward the patient's sense of guilt may sometimes seem offensive. The poor fellow confesses his list of sins and the analyst remains unmoved. Occasionally an analyst really does feel aloof listening to a patient reproaching himself.

One of my patients, a married man with several children, used to blame himself hour after hour for his erotic fantasies that blossomed out the moment he saw a beautiful woman on the street. This took place in Havana, where there were plenty of them. When I protested, saying that as far as I knew he had never been unfaithful, he dismissed me with a comment to the effect that as I wasn't a Christian I couldn't understand his guilt. Once, in passing, he mentioned that he saved money by giving low wages to his employees. Five dollars a month to the servants and 20 dollars to his chauffeur (who had a wife and child). I declared that the wages were too low. Furiously he accused me of being a Communist. Of course that was obvious, since I came from Sweden. At the end of the session I told him that perhaps guilt over erotic fantasies was easier to bear than the real sense of guilt he suffered from neglecting his social responsibilities. He did not reply, nor did he return to the subject. Toward the end of the month he told me with some embarrassment that he had raised the wages. They were now far above average. I didn't say anything. Any comment of mine would only have increased his feeling of shame.

Franz Alexander has traced the silent bargaining human beings conduct with their own conscience—"In accepting punishment the patient buys indulgences for the satisfaction or acting out of impulses, thereby making it possible for him to close his eyes to what happens. The patient's ego is also involved in the corrupt barter."

There is no contradiction whatsoever between Alexander's view of neurotic guilt and the outlook Sirnes expresses when he says: "A person who tries to brush aside his feeling of guilt and pretend that it doesn't exist is repressing his guilt. But it returns in the form of neurosis in the same way as other suppressed material. Yet perhaps the main reason for misunderstandings and the problem of guilt is that in the end there remain contradictions and ambiguities in analytic theory just as in life itself."

Freud created an essential part of his theory as a modern parallel to the drama of King Oedipus by Sophocles. The tragedy can be told in many ways, but basically it is a drama of man's reaction to natural catastrophe.

The people of Thebes suffer from famine because the land is plagued by a drought. Tiresias, the seer, recommends introspection. Among the Thebans there is a man whose guilt has not been expiated. Only after he has confessed his guilt will the gods send rain. The highest citizen of the state, the king, searches his soul and discovers his guilt. He has murdered his father and married his mother. But he never knew that the marauder he struck down in self-defense was his father. Nor did he know that the woman he loved was his mother. Oedipus has committed patricide and incest, yet he has never seen either his father or his mother. He was abandoned in a mountain wilderness when he was only a few days old. But the king of Thebes acknowledges his guilt before his suffering people. He blinds himself and goes into exile, followed by his two daughters,

who are also his sisters. Jocasta, his wife and mother, commits
suicide. Here the tragedy ends. Whether or not the king's sacrifice has appeased the gods remains an open question.

No one knows when it started to rain.

Man seems to have a deeply rooted tendency to feel guilty
when he is confronted by problems he is unable to solve. Oedipus was guilty because his parents had left him out in the
wilderness. In psychoanalytic treatment we see over and over
again that a child feels guilty when he realizes he is not loved
by his mother and father. This is indeed a natural catastrophe.

When, in his passionate defense of the undiminished importance of Christianity in modern society, Tollak Sirnes reduces
religion to depth psychology, he will hardly encounter any
opposition from the psychologists, although the conservative
theologians of the church might not agree with him: "We have
analyzed, psychologized and pathologized religion at the same
time as we've disregarded the fact that religion itself is a
psychology."

Like all great human documents, the Gospels have a timeless
scope which permits a minister to interpret them in precisely
the way he feels them, in the limited amount of time in which
he lives, to be relevant and important. Man does not live by
bread alone, says the Gospel of St. Matthew. The deep psychological knowledge that these words bear in a welfare state cannot be denied. When the most degrading material privations
have been abolished, perhaps then, for the first time in our
history, people who have never been able to afford the luxury of
spiritual life will feel an undefined psychic need, a need so bare
and elementary, so stripped of all ideology that it occasionally
will seem catastrophic. The Swedish controversy concerning
new ways and forms for disseminating culture is a promising
start toward meeting this unarticulated need. Mental hygiene
alone certainly cannot meet it.

It is easy for Sirnes to defend Christianity, because he draws
no line between the Gospels and the Christian church as an
organization. Even an atheist can appreciate the timeless beauty

of the Gospels, their humanity, their defense of the poor, the outlawed and the oppressed. But a nonbeliever cannot agree with the church and its dogmas. Religious institutions are far more conservative and much less open to reform and criticism than the secular institutions of a democratic state. Evidently the contradistinction between the Gospels' appeal for self-scrutiny and the stubborn resistance to self-criticism and change within Christian organizations cannot be resolved.

In October 1945 the Council of Twelve in the German Evangelical Church published a document called *Confession of Guilt, Stuttgart, 1945,* which begins with the words:

> However excruciating it may be to say so, it was because of us that endless suffering has been inflicted on many peoples and countries ... [It ends] Hence, at a moment when the whole world needs a new beginning we ask: *Veni, Creator Spiritus!* [Come, Creator Spirit].

This confession, in which the German language is resurrected from its degradation and tries to attain a simple Biblical tone, was never accepted by the German church. It was considered lacking in dignity and politically unwise.

"In truth," writes the German theologian H. Zarnt,[6] "it was an act of dignity and one of the most dignified moments in the history of postwar Germany, which otherwise is not especially well endowed with them."

At the second session of the Vatican Council in Rome in 1964, a proposal was discussed to offer atonement to the Jewish people for the murder of God. Bishop Bea tried to appease the bishops working in the Arab countries by pointing out that it was purely a religious suggestion and took no position on the question of whether the Vatican should recognize the state of Israel or at least prepare public opinion for such a possibility.

"Nevertheless, the section concerned was never brought to a vote nor was the section dealing with freedom of belief. The reactionary forces have apparently not loosened their grip," the Norwegian historian August Schou concluded.[7]

It is this unsavory mixture of current-day political considerations in an organization which claims at the same time to preach infallible truth that has made people oppose Christianity. They are opponents of the church and its dogmas, but hardly of the Gospels. During the sometimes bitter and unrelenting struggle, opponents of the church have often overlooked the progressive currents and stared their eyes out at the conservative majority, who may occasionally cause quite a commotion, and isolated reactionary elements. But the Swedish church isn't limited to Bishop Giertz and the Church Assembly. It contains as well such dissimilar personalities as Carl-Gustav Boëthius and Ludvig Jönsson, Curt Norell and Rune Pär Olofsson. And the cause of the blacks in South Africa is defended not only by author Per Wästberg but also by bishop Gunnar Helander.

Tollak Sirnes claims, perhaps somewhat polemically, that we would do very well to increase the number of hours allocated to religious instruction so that children and young people would acquire greater wisdom about life. The suggestion is probably relatively unimportant right now in both Sweden and Norway, but psychologists may have some reservations about the effort to abolish all religious instruction in schools. To a great extent the values and norms on which Nordic democracy is based are expressed in the language of the Christian religion. Secularized humanism has still not come up with a uniform, standard language, although obviously the schools should teach the various humanistic documents, be it the Communist Manifesto or the profane psalms by the poet Arnulf Överland. By and large the Christian doctrine in the Nordic countries today is devoted to the idea of peace and brotherhood. To me it seems unwise to remove such a deeply rooted popular ideology from the instruction in countries where the individual student is assured the freedom either to accept or to reject the faith he is brought up with.

Despite all his bantering atheism, Tryggve Bull, a fellow countryman of Tollak Sirnes and a Social Democrat in the Parliament, has a more realistic view of the part the church should play in a democratic state:

> Perhaps it is not worthy of a free people to seek consolation in a Savior who died in Palestine 2,000 years ago and who now is in

heaven, but nevertheless a remote Savior is better than a live one tyrannizing us today. If our society is making progress in terms of security and open-mindedness, we may then be sure that in one form or another "liberal trends" will emerge in the church. The active rationalists and psychologists who have fought the church and religious instruction directly will have had a share in bringing this about. But both the state church and religious instruction have such strong, deep roots in tradition that, realistically speaking, we would achieve much better and also speedier results if we helped reform these institutions gradually rather than try creating something totally new, "just" and "true."[8]

It seems to me that the demand for "objective instruction in Christianity" is a psychological absurdity and the best way to destroy the people's Christian tradition. A teacher who doesn't believe that what he is teaching is in itself of any value, whether it's arithmetic, French or religion, suffers from low self-esteem and does not inspire his pupils to take an interest in the subject. But if a teacher of Christianity doesn't believe the story of the good Samaritan, he isn't even a compassionate person. But I wonder whether children wouldn't believe it anyhow. A teacher who believes in what he has to offer doesn't scare anybody. But a teacher who threatens children with eternal damnation and hellfire makes his pupils fearful and uncertain. A person who threatens people is not a believer. He is afraid. Faith—regardless of its content—frees people from anguish. In Norway Bishop Kristian Schjelderup and later also the Church Department have put an end to this threat.

In the social-democratic newspaper *Stockholms-Tidningen* Gunnar Fredriksson has pointed out that the demand for objectivity in religious instruction fails on the grounds of its incongruity, because it deprives the teacher of the power of verbal communication.

The teacher who strives for objective instruction and moreover tries not to lose the instinctive qualities of Christianity has no language whatsoever to use. Either he provides only superficial knowledge or else he uses religious language, in which case he preaches religion and that is forbidden by the Parliament.

Tollak Sirnes is no one-sided fanatic. His defense of Christianity doesn't imply any condemnation of those who aren't believers. On the contrary, he believes

> there is a great difference between people who have a universal sense of morals and those who have none at all. We can deeply disagree as to what kind of morals are right, and to be sure it is not given any mortal to sit in judgment over this. A respect for the moral code of other people presupposes humility—those who know they are humble often give themselves away, but people who are confident about it are unaware of their ignorance.

I believe that Sirnes' defense of Christianity is based on his conviction that religious experience is one of the best guarantees for the preservation and protection of human dignity: "This feeling of being confronted by something holy and sacred is in my experience very propitious to mental health." The feeling that every person has something inviolable within him is firmly anchored to the Christian idea that God created man—all men —in his own image. All the best things in Christianity can be traced back to this universal concept.

For people to be able to speak different languages, and yet have one common mother tongue, is an inalienable democratic right.

Contrary to Sirnes, I believe that political democracy offers a firmer guarantee for the individual's freedom of movement than the organization represented by the church. It is far safer to be able to refer to a law which directs the dealings of people here on earth, because it has the quality of an objective reality. On the other hand, in a dangerous situation it is difficult to draw on religious experience no matter how convincing an inner truth it may contain. It is and remains ambiguous and unpredictable.

But the main thing I want to say here is that the experience which the church has always called its own and which has given us so much of our visual imagery, our symbols and our language isn't the exclusive property of those who are religious. It is a universal human experience of undeniable worth. In a state of ecstatic religious experience the individual has overcome his fear and conquered death. But in moments of extreme danger even the nonbeliever may triumph over his anguish and achieve a heroic, simple sense of dignity.

Ben Shahn has drawn a picture of two modest, extremely simple men, somewhat square and ungainly, looking a bit lost in life. Beneath their portrait Shahn has written the following original lines:

> If it had not been for these things, I might have lived out my life talking at street corners to scorning men. I might have died, unmarked, unknown, a failure. Now we are not a failure. This is our career and our triumph. Never in our full life could we hope to do such work for tolerance, for justice, for man's understanding of man as now we do by accident. Our words—our lives—our pains nothing! The taking of our lives—lives of a good shoemaker and a poor fish peddler—all! That last moment belongs to us—that agony is our triumph. [*Passion of Sacco and Vanzetti*, 1958, serigraph, collection of Ben Shahn.]

These words from the speech for the defense of Sacco and Vanzetti contain the same elements as those found in a religious experience, with an essential difference that we may, with Göran O. Eriksson, call "reduction." The element of objective reality remains untouched. Sacco and Vanzetti talk about accident where the believer would talk about Providence or God's will.

The human ability to respond—whether in a religious or a secular way—can be described as a feeling or a state of rapture (*Ergriffenheit*), to borrow an expression from the Swiss professor of psychology of religion, Kerenyi.[9] It occurs when a sensation is no longer bound to the secondary processes of consciousness but forces its way into deeper layers where primary processes are in command, independent of space and time. At such moments the objective nature of the sensation is transformed into a subjective one of timeless validity, and this becomes a permanent part of the personal identity. What is most striking about this sensation is the fact that the world is seen in terms of reversed values. Active endeavor is experienced as passive receptivity: subject and object change places. There is no longer any freedom of choice. On all these levels the ego has made a choice, but has experienced it passively as if it had been overwhelmed. There remains a sense of being chosen, and this undoubtedly makes one feel responsible.[10]

A person who has experienced the world from the point of view of reversed values achieves an astonishing release from anxiety and is even willing to pay a high price for it. Semmelweiss, who discovered childbed fever, did not receive any recognition during his lifetime. Finally he proved that his observations were correct by infecting himself and dying.

The truth has chosen me and not the other way around, says Kerenyi. Even the objective observations of a scientist must be transformed into subjective, psychic reality before they become wholly convincing.

Nor is the sensation unfamiliar to the artist. Certainly the ability to create is rooted deeply in one's personality, as a result of both one's constitution and one's experience. But the artist perceives his talent as total dedication to some compelling force outside himself, a force he is dependent on. This dependency may be so powerful that it blasts the language of religious symbols.

> Both in my life and my painting I can very well do without God, the Father, but in the midst of my suffering I cannot be without something that is greater than me and is my whole life: my ability to create. [Vincent van Gogh, the catalogue of the Modern Museum, October 1965.]

If the feeling of inspiration as a result of being chosen has always been considered essentially religious, no doubt it was due to the fact that religion first sanctioned it by veiling it in the universal symbolic language of primary processes. When the poet Arnold Ljungdal, who couldn't precisely be called a man of the church, starts to describe the transition from active to passive at the moment of creation, he suddenly uses religious language. "Because a sustaining grace rarely comes unexpectedly, it demands of the receiver not only a humble and expectant attitude. Without an active state of anticipation, which at the decisive moment supplies the necessary form of expression, no live work of art can come into being," he writes in the introduction to the Swedish version of the *Duino Elegies* of Rilke.[11]

The feeling that the roles of object and subject, receiver and giver are reversed is reserved not only for artists, scientists and believers. Among other things, it is an unconscious element in the appreciation of art—a feeling that I am not looking at the work of art; it is looking at me. An irresistible appeal to insight and renewal, a magic conviction that dream must become reality, emanates from a work of art as well.

In his poem "Torso of an Archaic Apollo," Rilke has described this experience. Like a powerful eye the classical torso peers at him, and the artfully shaped marble says to him, with relentless intensity: You must change your life!

> Never will we know his fabulous head
> where the eyes' apple slowly ripened. Yet
> his torso glows: a candlelabrum set
> before his gaze which is pushed back and hid,
> restrained and shining, . . . until there is no place
> that does not see you. You must change your life.

The will to change, the sense that an individual human being has an unlimited capacity for development, can be called the moral attraction of art, as long as "moral" is not taken here in the spirit of a kind of municipal warning (i.e., "Don't Be A Litterbug"). No, the appeal of art lies in its overpowering sense of certainty that all of us, each and every one, have the ability to make our lives meaningful, and that this resource, in all of us, is unlimited. Without this irrational linkage of the will, of a sense of values to insight and regeneration, secular humanism would amount to no more than a kind of moralistic tale listened to halfheartedly.

Humanität ist religiöse Verehrung des Geheimnisses, das sich in Menschen verkörpert. Seitdem der Mensch Mensch ist—ist er mehr als Natur. Diese Mehr gehört zu seiner Natur.

Thomas Mann, *Mass und Wert*, 1938

It seems to me that the time has come for secular humanism to liberate itself from the use of religious language and to formulate its own language out of the existing conditions, which would be on the same level and not in competition with the world of religious symbolism.

Göran O. Eriksson seems to be one of the few who have realized that the religious experience contains a psychological truth which should be transposed to secular usage even if it does undergo a certain reduction.

But I wonder whether religious experience can be reduced to carnal lust or the desire to create, without at the same time bringing about an incurable loneliness of the heart. Perhaps Göran O. Eriksson hasn't noticed that he contradicts himself when he claims that "the world is multiplicity in which for a moment each individual trait has the power to subdue all the others" (*Stockholms Tidningen* 2/11/65). He has adopted the religious language but kept the dimension of depth on a secular level.

Presumably the primary mother-child relationship is the foundation for the universal human experience of ecstasy in which a person openly accepts his presence in the world.

A mother protects and feeds the newborn baby. But at some rare moments she sees the infant spread its arms and embrace her. The child's winning smile encompasses her and she is struck by a feeling of happiness and unlimited gratitude: "A child is born in Bethlehem. . . . A child is born in every home," Arnulf Överland once sang. People fall on their knees before the child, the world of tomorrow, the promise at dawn. They bow to a sense of "uniqueness" which at an ecstatic moment dares to experience a world of reversed values.

Today's secular language of symbols seems to have lost the immediate naïveté of religious symbols. It has become more abstract, more impersonal. But whatever form it may take, it is a contribution to the human will to live and regenerate, a contribution we cannot do without.

1965

4. CRISIS OF TRUST AND ALIENATION

in memory of René de Monchy

We all know from our personal experience that we can be ourselves only in and through our world and there is a sense in which "our" world will die with us, although "the world" will go on without us.

—R. D. LAING

R OBERT COLES, the psychiatrist and psychoanalyst, was born and bred in New England, where the pioneer spirit of his freedom-seeking ancestors has become a traditional obligation, an aristocrat who knows that nobility obliges. "I have tried," he says, "to carry psychiatric study into an active social struggle."[1] He moved to the South and became staff psychiatrist of the Student Nonviolent Coordinating Committee (SNCC). He visited people who had been arrested and put in jail and treated them for episodes of anxiety, insomnia, borderline psychosis and depression. He led therapy groups of students who were active in the struggle. His main problem was to understand why some of them became disillusioned, indifferent and weary of defending their own and other people's lives. The work of these students consisted not only of the activities that are captured on film or referred to in the news. Their main efforts were directed at securing a foothold in the cities where their goals, at best, were considered illegal or disruptive of the general order. The blacks in the Southern cities were deeply apathetic, to a great extent they lacked formal education, and most of them were apprehensive and afraid of all expressions of protest concerned with their own rights.

The experience of encountering suspicion among people you

are fighting for or, as in the case of the black youth, finding it among your own people weakens the fighting spirit and undermines psychic balance. The naïve idealism of the young people and their obvious desire to sacrifice their lives and their futures in the cause of the oppressed threatened to break down when they were confronted with grim reality. They had expected open arms and boundless loyalty. Instead they met with indignation and found people suspiciously turning their backs to them. Many of the struggling young people never gained sober social and psychological insight into the fact that the suspicion of the older people and especially of the elderly blacks was based on the attitude of the oppressors and the submission of the oppressed, as well as on the fear they both had, although for different reasons. But when the young blacks, in their bitterness, confusion and painful disappointment, turned to the chief psychiatrist for help, their own suspicions emerged. Their own sense of inferiority, which they had denied, flared up into a feeling of hate and envy which threatened to destroy the minimum of confidence necessary for a therapeutic working relation.

> Many of them are profoundly suspicious of outsiders, even those recommended to them by their fellows; and I am white, which is an obstacle for many Southern Negroes who need time and experience to feel even remotely comfortable with *any* white person, even those who stand beside them in demonstrations, let alone a watching psychiatrist.[2]

But Coles continues by saying that the suspicion and aloofness soon gave way to the sound relationship that developed between him and his students and associates.

Another American analyst, Viola Bernard, has written a penetrating study[3] about the credibility crisis a black patient goes through in his relation to a white therapist.

I read this account with a gnawing sense of concern. It displayed a change in the atmosphere of the psychoanalytic situation which went against everything I had considered necessary —in a silent, unspoken way—for all psychotherapeutic work.

I am not unfamiliar with tense relations between a minority group and the majority of a population. But to me it always seemed obvious that the therapeutic situation stood apart, was a kind of oasis, where such hostility was not operative. There was a silent agreement between both parties that social conventions and prejudices were banned. It was simply a situation between two people who were trying to clear up the difficulties one of them had. If the other—that is to say, the psychoanalyst —was properly analyzed and, like Augustinus, knew the jealousy a child feels when he sees his brother suckling at his mother's breast, then the therapeutic process could go on of its own accord.

Perhaps my naïveté was due to an innocence that James Baldwin has so relentlessly attacked:

> What most whites imagine they can save in the face of life's storms is basically their innocence—most whites I have known have given me the impression that they are imprisoned in a rare nostalgia, in a dream of a past era of security and order, a dream on which they have inevitably and unconsciously staked their life and often lost it.[4]

I have asked myself whether my naïveté as a psychoanalyst consisted of believing that everyone has an inborn ability to feel immediate human intimacy. I had not taken into account people who live their lives in a state of coldness and suspicion and who, unlike neurotics, have accepted this. When I look back upon my practice as a psychoanalyst, I certainly must admit that in daily clinical work I seem gradually to have lost my innocence and that perhaps a long time ago I accepted not only the patient's but also the therapist's fundamental aloneness. It is only that a dream always lasts much longer than the facts of the everyday reality we live with. And this may have its advantages.[5]

One's own analysis and a life rich in experiences are the unquestionable conditions for psychoanalytic work. But the special clientele I encountered in Stockholm as a beginner during the years of the last war confronted me with a world I was not prepared to meet, a world governed by death, where the only way to survive was by "getting accustomed to death,"[6] a world where nothing was more dangerous than to come close to having hope. Even the slightest glimpse of a possibility of freedom, which could ignite a weak, flickering light in the life of a concentration-camp prisoner, could become his downfall. Psychoanalyzing people with such an experience in their very recent past compelled me to take a number of conscious measures—which today are self-evident—against the conventional practice and made me especially sensitive to the fundamental change which occurred in psychoanalytic theory after the Second World War, but from which I was cut off for many years. This isolation also had its advantages. This development did not come to me by means of *Lesefrüchte* (book learning). I had to live through the change with my patients.

When one of these patients came in, he could move confidently and naturally into the room and say a friendly hello to me, but as soon as he lay down on the couch, the atmosphere changed in a ghostly fashion. His body would sink down and grow weak and he had no control over it. His voice would become monotonous and he'd start to mumble. He talked without punctuation, without start or finish—endlessly reiterating scenes of torture and mistreatment—unaware of time and place, forgetting that there was someone listening to him. He didn't feel that I was in the room, sitting behind him. When the session was over, he'd slip away flat, shadowlike, and nod his head slightly without looking around. I realized that I would have to seat the patient in a chair in front of me so he couldn't forget my presence. I also learned that under certain circumstances psychopathological reactions, such as depersonalization, for instance, may have a life-sustaining function. I was able to observe and feel that people can actually be degraded into lifeless, severely damaged objects, that consciousness of one's own identity can be reduced to the minimum, to a number imprinted on the arm. But I also saw emotional intensity even when their bonds with people had ceased to exist, that the loss of a safety pin could cause anguish, tears, and a general sense of disorientation.[7] I started to realize that there were cases where the psychoanalyst was not only an unconscious parent figure for the patient but also something totally new: a person who could bridge the gap between the loss of identity as well as death and the multiplicity of existence, *la joie de vivre*.

It started to dawn on me that language was no simple instrument in human communication. The mother tongue of many of my patients was Yiddish, Czech or Polish. One day I heard myself talking to them in perfect High German. It didn't sound very good to my ears. It was like the correct, impersonal German used by the prison guards. Now, when I think back on these therapies, I believe the patients didn't express fully their pent-up feelings of hatred and rage toward their oppressors because of the therapist's—that is to say, my—faultless German.

Some 20 years later—starting in 1963—I had some patients in therapy who had been released from concentration camps when they were teenagers. An old analytic rule says that it is preferable to analyze the patient in his mother tongue. But neither my patients nor I felt any need to speak German. They spoke Swedish very well and had nothing against listening to my mixture of Norwegian and Swedish. When I occasionally said something in German, they answered in Swedish. Evidently a person prefers to speak the language he feels most confident with and that guarantees a direct, positive contact with people. But the language he chooses doesn't always have to be his mother tongue. (Language is part of a person's life style, and even that can be fundamentally changed.)

Gradually I began to realize that depersonalization can be more than a defense mechanism, that it is—or it was—the whole existence of my patients, and that the quality of my feeling alive was completely different from theirs. They had become things: mute, immobile, dead.

My therapeutic optimism cooled somewhat and I started saying to my patients: "Tell me! Tell me not only about your symptoms but also about how you experience the world, what it seems like to you. I don't know you, you see. My world is different from the one you live in. But if you describe, in detail, what your experiences are like, maybe I will be able to grasp something of the special atmosphere that surrounds your life and that no one can share with you completely. I don't want to get to know merely your motives; I want to know how you deal with your experiences and how you function within the framework of your own personality."

A purely phenomenological description of details on the psychic surface, something we have earlier been able to neglect, is essential and especially meaningful for ego psychology, Heinz Hartmann wrote in 1953.[8]

In the early 1950s people who in many ways resembled refugees entered psychoanalytic treatment. They were strangers in their own land, in their own environment, and they were also strangers in relation to themselves. Of course, they had a vague sense that something was amiss, but they didn't know what it was. They had largely accepted the feeling of emptiness and formlessness as well as a pervading passive attitude toward life. Life went its own little way, but they were not aware of playing an active part in it. The lassitude and poverty of their inner sensations was most characteristic. The patients complained that, even though they were conscious of their feelings and their identity, they felt strange. They could not understand that what happened to them actually concerned them. Even though they had an integrated ego sense, they could not handle it. Neither their emotional nor their intellectual experiences could be related to a permanent identity.

While depersonalized man suffers from far-reaching neurotic conflicts of ambivalence that swing from suicidal impulses to homicidal ones, alienated people suffer from a disturbance in ego development without necessarily having any instinctual conflicts. It is a striking fact that alienated patients often function in a satisfactory way sexually. However, patients who suffer from neuroses are always troubled by sexual problems. Nevertheless, the neurotic person has a clearly defined sense of his own identity and a definite desire to get well, that is to say, to bring about a dynamic change in the conditions of his life.

The alienated person's inner world, which is so inaccessible to someone standing in the midst of life, is timeless. The alarm goes off in the morning and it goes off at night and not much happens in between. Imperceptibly days and nights flow into each other in the steady stream of an undefined present. There is no past and no future. The alienated person lives in a world without trust. Samuel Beckett, who because of the Gestapo spent some time in solitary confinement, has described this world. In it death has lost its meaning: it is neither an enemy nor a friend. It seems to be beyond the pain of transience, which is our fate. We live, said Rilke, and are always taking leave. The alienated person does not take leave. But his rootlessness makes us feel ill-at-ease. Maybe it seems familiar. When it comes down to basics, then we also are mere chance occurrences that soon pass away. *"Denn wir haben hier keine bleibende Statt,"* says Brahms' *Requiem.*

Bengt Nerman,[9] who has an unusual ability to describe the steadily flowing experiential structure of alienation, considers the unreal situation of language the starting point for the disorientation of alienated people. Words—things—people do not exist as isolated phenomena, because "words do not come into contact with sensations and therefore can never be experienced as real. The sensation does not acquire a gestalt in me, which means that I myself have no characteristics. I do not participate in what happens: I lack time. But that is the same as saying: I live without death."

In this elusive world the function of language is transformed, and this can cause a number of misunderstandings in therapeutic communication. A patient may talk about an event which the analyst thinks happened several days before. After some time it becomes apparent that it occurred ten years ago. Another patient may speak somewhat vaguely about an occurrence, as if it had taken place a long time ago and he was having a hard time reconstructing it. In the end we find out that it had happened on his way to the session.

We often notice that a patient never says "I," but instead uses an impersonal pronoun or some other circumlocution. Or he switches around the active and passive voices. "And so it was done," a young woman often said to me and could not understand why every time I answered her by saying, "And you did it." The sense of being an instrument that circumstances toy with is one of the main characteristics of the way an alienated person experiences the world.

Sometimes I was surprised at my spontaneous interpretation of a patient's expression. I tried to make it normal by adding the word "like." A patient complained that he was an amoeba. The man was diligent in his work; he was married and had several children. At first sight he didn't seem to me at all like an amoeba. One day I told him that it was difficult for me to understand how he could feel he was like an amoeba. "No," he said firmly, "I don't feel like an amoeba, I *am* an amoeba." I perceived that the word "like" was my own protection against sensing an inner world which in its frozen silence and lack of spontaneous mobility was very different from my own.

It has often been pointed out that misunderstanding alienated patients does not offend them. I have had the same experience. One patient talked for a long time about the dead. I was very captivated by this and listened eagerly. Some time passed and once, when I made some comments, he looked at me in surprise, like a person who suddenly wakes from a dream, and said: "Why, you talk about them as if they were really dead—but my dead people are alive." When we talked about death, he meant his own inner life, an eternal life, a state of tensionless Nirvana.

Among other things, it is the special archaic use of language —which often has a surprising lyric beauty—that distinguishes the alienated disturbance of the ego from the neurotic depersonalization. Depersonalized people have at their command a much more "adult" usage of language, that is to say, they are more at ease with secondary processes than alienated people are.

The uncommon tolerance of alienated people is explained by their loneliness and isolation. They have more or less given up hope of being understood—if they have ever had any. But they also live in a world in which the function of language as a medium of communication is of minor importance. The sound of a word, the tone of a voice, the changes in the face of the person who is speaking, the shades of lighting in the room are their way of making contact.

Several times in the course of a conversation one alienated patient looked uneasily toward the window. It was clear that he seemed troubled. Finally he got up, without saying anything, and started to straighten out a tangled heap of electric cords that were lying on the floor. Then he came back and sat down. I looked at him questioningly. "A little anxious," he answered in a friendly, though apologetic way.

I have always liked clear-cut opinions, the advice the Bible gives: "But let your communication be Yea, yea; nay, nay: for whatsoever is more than these cometh of evil." This has seemed the most natural thing to me. Thus, I have occasionally felt impatient with some of my patients who have not been able to say right off what was bothering them, but who instead concealed their problems and came up with insinuations. Finally I made a virtue of necessity and asked them kindly to express themselves clearly, because unfortunately I lacked the ability to comprehend understatements that were all too subtle. In this instance, too, I had the same experience. The patients were not offended; rather, they did their best to make themselves understood. This had an unexpected therapeutic effect: the patients started to make verbal contact on the level of secondary processes, that is to say of ordinary consciousness. But by the very fact that they made themselves understood by another person, they also became clearer and more significant to themselves, more aware of their own authenticity.

Psychoanalysts who, like myself, are trained in treating classical neuroses may easily make a mistake that adds to the difficulty of the therapeutic work. We are led to believe that the patient's vagueness and formlessness is a lack of trust in the analyst. He wants to mislead the therapist and finds himself in a state of negative transference. But the alienated patient has no choice. He has only this extremely inadequate way of conveying his feelings. His vagueness is not conscious manipulation. He *is* vague. As a matter of fact, the psychoanalyst is the only person to whom the patient dares show how rootless his existence is. On the surface he often hides behind a facade of routine activities that keeps the people he meets at a distance and stands in the way of genuinely spontaneous human contact.

Far from being an obstacle, my apparent difficulties in entering an alienated person's existence seemed at any rate to guarantee the patient his own minimum identity. These people felt that a spontaneous, intuitive understanding was a dangerous intimacy that might shatter their own fragile personality structure. Reluctantly I began to realize that the alienated person does not long for immediate human intimacy. He shuns it as though it were a threat to his life.

My encounter with alienated persons forced me to perceive my own limitations in delving into the patient's inner world. I could no longer say, "What you're feeling just now—I've felt that way too, a long time ago." Without an assuring "I know," I came to realize that the first step in understanding the patient was to perceive my own strangeness to him, my existential difference. I was extremely dependent on the patient's cooperation, his patience and endurance.

Even though it was frustrating to experience the alienated patient's coolness—his lack of desire for spontaneous human contact—this taught me something about the problem of countertransference. The patient reacted to a very withdrawn attitude with suppressed enmity and absurd transference fantasies. But the extent to which I could be myself with the patient depended on the degree of his health—not his pathology. It may have been this discovery more than anything else that clarified for me the fact that the autonomy of a therapist is an illusion. The psychotherapeutic process does not take place outside ordinary human contacts; it can function only in a state of mutual dependency.

I was not the only one to feel the need for reorientation. The psychoanalytic literature of the 1950s is filled with a revived discussion of the relationship between patient and analyst and a reevaluation of the psychotherapeutic situation in its entirety. It started with a comprehensive discussion of the analyst's countertransference and initiated what I would call a "continuous democratization" of psychoanalytic work.

Margaret Little, one of the many unconventional and highly original British psychoanalysts, opened the discussion and effectively torpedoed the analyst's attitude of splendid isolation in relation to the patients:

> So much emphasis is laid on the unconscious fantasies of patients about their analysts that it is often ignored that they really come to know a great deal of truth about them—both actual and psychic. . . . Analysts often behave unconsciously exactly like the parents who put up a smoke screen, and tantalize their children, tempting them to see the very things they forbid their seeing.[10]

Merit Hertzman-Ericson[11] believes that the patient tends to communicate spontaneously in proportion to his faith in the therapist, and this is made easier by ordinary, open and "unmystical" contact.

By stepping down from his invisible throne and renouncing his magic and authoritative weight, the analyst also had to relinquish his categorical demand that the patient at any cost stick to the analytic rule: You must tell me absolutely everything! Instead, he gave the patient the freedom to decide for himself what he wished to convey. Little writes:

> We no longer "require" our patients to tell us all that is in their minds. On the other hand, we give them permission to do so. . . .
>
> In the old days analysts, like parents, said what they liked when they liked, as by right, and the patients had to take it. Now, in return for the permission to speak or withhold freely, we ask our patients to allow us to say some things, and allow them too to refuse them.[12]

What and how much the patient conveys to us depends on how much confidence he has in his psychoanalyst. This free will of the patient could not have blossomed so long as the psychoanalyst put pressure on the patient's conscience. I believe that a more democratic, tolerant attitude toward the patient has eased this pressure and reduced his anxiety as well as his tendency to have deep depressions involving a suicide risk, which was common in the analyses of earlier times. The new sense of free will and mutual dependence has also liberated the patient's creative abilities. Psychoanalytic treatment today has become a positive, dynamic process, an inner rehabilitation which gives a sense of liberation. But the psychoanalyst has also felt good, because the treatment has become more comprehensive and subtle as it has been focused on the patient's whole existence and not only on its psychopathological aspects. Psychoanalysts have acquired a more interesting and exciting profession than their colleagues had before them.[13] They often complained that very little happened during treatment—what they didn't realize was that when they forced themselves to become a mirror, the patients did the same and were as bored as the analysts. In the 1930s and 1940s analysts were often worried over the fact that patients were so uncommunicative and might remain completely silent for long periods of time. Silence as a form of resistance can, as far as I can see, be said to have disappeared completely from psychoanalysis. But good, calm, creative silence—this remains.

At the moment it is fashionable to ridicule psychoanalysts of the older school. In doing this, people totally disregard the fact that their highly developed self-discipline and endless patience created the system of objective data concerning the development of man's instincts which today we build upon when we place the study of interpersonal relations at the center of psychoanalytic therapy. Concentration on the expression of instincts forced the analyst to go back and discover the human tendency of regression. The study of object relations opened his eyes to man's need to move forward, to mature. This is why the basic tone of psychoanalysis in our day is incomparably more optimistic. Anna Freud writes:

> We find . . . that no two of a given analyst's patients are handled by him in precisely the same manner. With some patients we remain

deadly serious, with others humor or even jokes may play a part
. . . ; there are differences in the ways in which we receive and send
off patients, and in the degree to which we permit a real relationship to the patient to coexist with the transferred, fantasied one;
there is, even within the strictness of the analytic setting, a varying
amount of ease felt by analyst and patient. These wholly unin-
tended and unplanned variations in our responses are imposed on
us, I believe, not so much by the patients' neuroses but by the individual nuances of their personalities which may escape unobserved
otherwise. In the personal pressure which the patient exerts on us
in this manner, he betrays the subtleties of his healthy personality,
the degree of maturity reached by his ego, his capacity to sublimate,
his intellectual gifts, and his ability to view his conflicts at least
momentarily in an objective manner.[14]

In the beginning of the 1960s the patient and the analyst
finally acknowledged their mutual dependencies.

"I try," says R. D. Laing, "to recognize the patient as the
person he considers himself to be and wait for the patient in
turn gradually to recognize me as the person I consider
myself."[15]

Psychoanalytic treatment—that is to say, psychoanalyst
versus patient—has become a therapeutic working alliance. The
new word designates a fundamental change in the climate of
psychoanalytic theory and of the psychoanalyst's office.

A number of obscure points in psychoanalytic technique have
come up in connection with this new orientation: is the patient's
behavior in the psychoanalytic situation an expression of a
permanent state and should it be described, or is it an expression of a dynamic conflict which becomes immediately apparent
because of his relationship to the therapist and should it therefore be interpreted? The study of neuroses, when it came to
the understanding of this dynamic conflict, yielded a rich har-
vest. Research into the alienated person's more static world
created the concepts of structure and style. The study of children over a long period of time (from infancy to school age)

showed that "not a single behavior has remained the same, yet one is struck by the inherent continuity of behavioral style and of the child's pattern of adaptation."[16]

Continuity in the special manner people have of attacking problems and eventually solving them—whatever their content —forms an essential part of identity. Heinz Hartmann laid the groundwork for structural research when he established the fact that we have at our disposal a "basic human adaptive equipment" which is relatively independent of instinctual conflicts. Erik Erikson[17] has proved that a person's sense of identity is a product of ego development, which continues long after the development of the instincts has ended.

When people became interested in the structure and style of individual personality, they could not avoid being particularly interested in the cognitive functions of the ego. Just after the Second World War a new school was formed in the field of the psychology of perception: it was "The New Look," headed by Blake and Klein.[18] Their experiments illustrated how man's affects and needs influence his perception, that is to say, the way in which he experiences the world around him. There are no objective sense perceptions. They are all interpreted from the very first moment. Generally this interpretation remains constant. But within this framework important modifications take place in relation to the individual's various ages. Perceptions are influenced only indirectly by need and motivation, for they pass through a structure that controls and regulates the impressions coming from the outside. David Shapiro— psychoanalyst and Rorschach specialist—says that an individual's "style" consists of "relatively stable and characteristic modes of functioning"[19] that transform external stimuli into subjective experience and manifest behavior. He concludes:

> It is only in the context of this subjective world or of these ways of functioning that the individual significance of any given mental content can be clearly understood. A mental content or a symptom, for instance, not only reflects the content of an instinctual impulse or counter impulse, but also it is a product of a style of functioning.

It is only when we understand the style and the general tendency of the individual's mind and interest that we can reconstruct the subjective meaning of the content of an item of behavior or thought. Without this understanding we run the risk—and it holds for therapists and testers alike—of seeing only textbook meanings, possibly correct but far removed from the sense and tone of an individual's experience.[20]

Now the difference between depersonalization and alienation —as I have described it here—also becomes clearer. Depersonalized people suffer from an unresolved conflict of ambivalence that oscillates between murder and suicide; frequently as children an older sister or brother, but never—as far as I can see—an adult, attempted to murder them. Their symptoms stem from a childhood trauma that is deeply suppressed. Their anxiety has nothing to do with their daily adult life and is therefore irrational. A dynamic conflict is enclosed in their symptom, a force that wants to emerge, to reach out to another person. It may be charged with too much aggressiveness or be directed toward the wrong object. But it is constantly in motion. At all times the main problem is: *how* do you achieve a contact that you long for, even though you deny it? But the depersonalized person's uncommon separation from outer reality forms a point of transition to an alienated personality.[21]

Alienated people suffer from no dynamic conflicts. The force that moves from within them out into the world is often somewhat weak and groping for unclear goals. In relation to the alienated a disturbing question arises: does the patient by and large *want* to establish contact? In which case, on what level? With things, animals or human beings? Nor is the anxiety of alienated persons always irrational, without foundation. Their ego is not sufficiently developed, and they have difficulties in manipulating themselves, let alone their environment.

Depersonalization and alienation set the psychoanalyst different tasks: on the one hand, the treatment of an unconscious, dynamic conflict in an otherwise fully developed personality and, on the other, the treatment of an insufficiently differentiated structure in a relatively undeveloped personality. The first case comprises the field of classic psychoanalysis. The other is new and has brought the problem of identity to the foreground.

We may ask ourselves why all this fuss is made over identity. Is it not a luxury that we may allow ourselves but which, strictly speaking, we don't need? Why, people do function without asking how they feel all the time and who they are.

First of all, we can answer that identity is indeed a luxury! For those who are not starving! People who are hungry have no identity or only an indistinct one. One of my first patients reminded me of the fact that my profession is useless for hungry people.

A metal worker who had lost his job because of a homosexual relationship with a younger fellow worker came to treatment because he wanted to overcome his sexual preference, which had created such difficult social problems for him. When he was lying on the couch he was always feeble and motionless and said very little in his quiet, affectless voice. The whole person was incomprehensible to me. He seemed frozen and weightless. The part most alive in this man was his dreams: they were filled with oral symbolism, but were also strangely diffuse, even though tangible. One day, after he had again told me such a dream, I asked him suddenly: "Did you have breakfast today?" No, he answered. "How did you get here?" "I walked," he said. "It takes an hour." It turned out that he was constantly tired and somewhat hungry and that he didn't have money for the busfare and he didn't dare accept any welfare because he didn't want to say why he was jobless. We agreed that he postpone the treatment until he had found a job. After two months he came back, quite changed. It was no longer difficult to form an opinion of his personality. He was working, eating and drinking, and feeling somewhat secure. His problem was still there. But now he met the essential requirement for solving it: he wasn't hungry.

Identity—a luxury of the well-fed? Very well. But let us then agree that it is perverse and degrading to live in a state of constant hunger. In today's welfare states it should be self-evident to assume that people have enough to eat, although in many parts of the world this is far from being true.

Today the preoccupation among psychotherapists of all schools with the question of identity is largely a result of the fact that a person's identity functions as his special sense organ coordinating various impressions. It is our most valuable instrument for perceiving our own existence. The instrument of identity has its own continuity, while at the same time it is in a state of constant flux.

> For our own past is covered by the currents of action . . .
> You are not the same person who left that station
> Or who will arrive at any terminus.[22]

A person's identity makes him capable of experiencing his existence not as a dead mirror image but as a space that he can demarcate for himself and where he can move toward definite goals.

The most interesting thing about the sense of identity is that it is both symbiotic and directed toward an object. Harold F. Searles[23] believes that a child who has not had a happy symbiotic relationship with his mother will be disturbed in his sense of identity. He is unable to grow away from her and become an independently functioning whole. The disturbance occurs if the mother denies the child a symbiotic relationship because she likes being the cosmos. The loss of the child infringes on her identity. She feels she is at the mercy of an unfathomable and pitiless world outside her. But problems may also come up on another level. A child cannot develop his own identity if he doesn't first clash with his mother's identity. The more courage the mother—and later on also the father—has to be herself, the easier it will be for the child to do likewise. This process of differentiation is mutual and almost never takes place without friction. The mother must realize that the child is an individual, on his own, with his personal rights as well as his own likes and dislikes. But the child also has to learn to respect the mother's right to exist and function as the person she is. Such development is hardly possible without many fits and starts on both sides. If all goes relatively well, the child will have learned to use his aggressiveness for constructive ends.

In analyzing people with identity disturbances, one occasionally notices that a patient reacts vehemently and unreasonably to the least thing you say. He seems to mobilize all his strength in order to resist the temptation to give up his own identity and live symbiotically with the psychoanalyst. Here, if anywhere, silence has its place, a calm, observing silence that gives the patient time to collect himself without having to defend himself against intruders.

On the other hand, it is clear that the analyst—like the mother—must have the courage to remain himself in his identity as analyst and not to be tempted to "step out of his professional role" and offer immediate satisfaction. To act like a parent would be a fictitious identity and not in the best interest of the patient. Sooner or later this would end in a mutual disappointment. No, the continuity of the contact lies in the fact that the analyst always remains himself and, if necessary, also bars himself from the patient's intrusion and absurd demands. The analyst is himself to the extent that he has found a personal style. He is no living textbook on the theory of neurosis, but a human being who passes on his knowledge and handles his technique in a personal way. A psychoanalyst's style is the history of the fusion of his theoretical as well as clinical knowledge and his entire life experience. Rudolf Löwenstein, who belongs to the classical school of psychoanalysis, believes that it takes ten years to develop a personal psychoanalytic style.

In brief: if the patient has encountered an inadequate or nonexistent identity in his parents, then he will find it in his analyst's way of handling the treatment, in his style and self-evident, firm professional identity, which in itself should be flexible and—preferably—comprehensive.

I recall gratefully my own psychoanalyst's style: his calm, unassuming dignity, the sudden flashes of humor and irony, his reluctance to use big words, his ability to discern a swarm of details and see the main features of an event, the convincing simplicity of his interpretations, the generous and unsophisticated acceptance of everything you said, his therapeutic patience and his wordless assurance. The only thing that I couldn't accept was the constant disorder on his desk. I would have been glad to become like him. But it didn't work out that way. In time I acquired my own style.

When we consider that a person's identity enters into the exchange between generations, that it is a process of both fusion and differentiation, we are also inclined to see the very serious problems of today's youth from a far wider perspective.

We have given young people unheard-of freedom. In return we demand that they know who they are, where they are going and how they are going to use their freedom. But every so often we meet formless individuals who have no tenable identity and who frequently behave in a contradictory and chaotic manner. But then we shouldn't forget that the parents of many of these young people were not able to offer their children a personal identity to grapple with. Such parents need not be psychically disturbed at all. But they grew up in a time when a personal attitude toward life was at best not required, was often undesirable or an absolute risk. It will take several generations before the sense of an individual identity becomes common property. In the meantime, we must put up with people who have no identity or, worse, who still have fluctuating identities or pseudo-identities and whose fickleness may cause trouble—an unforeseen weight in the balance of security within a democratic society.

Language is the instrument of the process of individuation. When a child can refer to himself as "I" and to his mother as "you," the process is completed. But above all language has been an instrument of the upper class, which also has always had the largest vocabulary. The common people have been silent—quite literally so. They have lived on the strength of their muscles and haven't needed many words. That time is now past. Only a dwindling few can live on physical strength alone. Modern education is related closely to language. The mass media makes words available to everyone, preferably alongside a picture. The general access to language will automatically increase an individual's vocabulary—regardless of his social group. So far we can be optimistic. If a person has words, he also has the prerequisite for developing identity.

In many other ways the treatment of alienated people also became the touchstone of the analyst's ability to learn all over again. The alienated may hurt another person and repel him unintentionally. He respects neither himself nor anyone else. His indifference can be taken as aggressiveness, though it need not be that at all. Freud writes that he became irritated when a patient came into his office for the first time and did not close the door behind him. He felt that the patient expressed contempt for the treatment he had to offer: it didn't matter if the door remained open; nothing important would be said here anyhow. But it might also be a blind, automatic way of adjusting to anyone and any situation, which E. G. Schachtel[24] believes is a striking feature of the alienated patient. Such a patient often does not feel that he has anything unique to say, or anything that belongs only to him and that he would want to keep from being observed by others. Perhaps he has not been able to enclose his inner world, nor has he developed a feeling of intimacy that Erikson rightly associates with the sense of identity. He has never learned to choose a person he can trust. One person is just as good as another—all cats are gray, etc. Alienated people have a weakly developed sense of quality and therefore are hardly selective. To an outsider it may seem like tolerance. But it doesn't fulfill the conditions of authentic tolerance: here I am and there you are and we're going to respect each other's differences. To strike this highly integrated balancing act between an individual demarcation and an appreciation of the differences in another person demands a clearly developed sense of one's own identity and a certain degree of self-respect, which is exactly what the alienated person lacks. In one of Georges Bernanos' novels, a country priest, who after a night of inner struggle gives permission for a football match to take place, says, "We have to love ourselves humbly."

The alienated patient's obvious openness need not be a sign of confidence in the therapist. An alienated person can be "open" with nearly anyone. Of course, he's not aware that he's communicating anything important. His inner and outer worlds are both equally unstructured and desolate. Such a discovery can be quite frustrating for the therapist. A person starts to acquire a certain sense of relativity in evaluating human actions. The core of a person's identity, for example, may consist of an experience during childhood when he lied and the adults did not notice. Lies—conscious lies—may form the beginning of the insight that there is a personal world inside you nobody else knows about. The secrets of a child—which adults have forgotten a long time ago—may be the core in the individual's sense of his identity. Gradually the child discovers that he can communicate his secrets to others, but he may also keep them to himself. Here the ability to choose, which is a highly developed ego function, makes its appearance. But even if a child is open and communicative, he has a growing sense that he can perceive his own secrets better than an adult ever could. To protect a child or a patient from the feeling of inescapable loneliness by requesting him to communicate everything is to work against his sense of identity as a unique being. A person who communicates with anyone at all at any time easily loses his sense of distance and gets on people's nerves. The comment of one character I saw in a cartoon the other day is revealing:

"She says his life is like an open book. The sad thing is that he insists on reading it out loud."

Sometimes a person will call on me saying that he wants to begin treatment. Once when I asked why me in particular, the person answered: "Well, you have such a nice parking place right outside the house." I can never get over his motivation. Here a person is about to confide his life and his future, his innermost anguish and his most secret hopes to another person and he doesn't seem to care what that other person is like and what impression he himself makes on her. Instead he depersonalizes the therapist-to-be and reduces her to an object—a thing.

My psychoanalytic training has taught me to tolerate a patient's transference in order to be able to represent the most diverse personalities he has met in his childhood. But I have not learned to represent a nonhuman environment. I had to give up my illusion that an analyst has an unlimited ability to handle a patient's transference. I draw the line between people and things. I cannot nor do I want to represent a parking lot. Psychoanalysts such as Winnicott, Little, Laing and Searles, for example, who have worked with schizophrenic patients, have taken a step out into a nonhuman environment in order to reach these patients who have lost all their faith in human relations and turned to animals and inanimate objects. But a schizophrenic will not "reduce" his therapist by aggressive action. He may not be able to perceive his existence on a human level because he has never reached it or has once and for all relinquished it.

It was a point of honor among the first generation of analysts to be able to treat any patients. The more competent you were, the more you could look beyond yourself to the benefit of the patient, the more you succeeded in becoming a big, benevolent ear, the greater ability you had to see the most diverse people. This is a tempting psychoanalytic ideal and a difficult one to dismiss. After many agonizing years, I have realized that for a therapist it is not an absolute ideal but a relative one. The psychoanalyst must strike a balance between an all too personally restricted choice and an impersonal boundlessness as well as a lack of selectivity. I read the comments of the Boston Psychoanalytic Institute in connection with a study of patients who had been treated by its trainees.

> Our work suggests the impossibility of treating patients as an aggregate of unrelated and separate qualities, and the difficulty, not to say impossibility, of carrying out most studies of this kind by evaluation of patients alone. The attributes and experience of the analyst, the establishment of the analytic situation, and finally the development and resolution of the transference neurosis must be taken into consideration.[25]

The right person in the right place, or a certain analyst feeling most comfortable with a certain patient and vice versa, seems to be a sensible modification in the omnivorous ideal, a modification which would reduce considerably the number of unsatisfactory results in psychoanalytic treatment.

The strategy of referral is a new, exciting and largely unexplored area within psychoanalytic theory. We soon discover that an opinion concerning the patient's chances of being treated with relative success cannot be an absolute factor. It must be seen in connection with the supply and demand of therapists, their own personalities and special talents. Therefore the patient's prospects for a successful treatment are functionally linked to the availability and choice of therapists. Sometimes we can refer very sick people—borderline psychotic cases—to a psychotherapist with a special interest in such cases and a record of having had good results in treating them, while we have a hard time finding a suitable therapist for an ordinary neurotic patient with a good prognosis because his personality and cultural background do not agree very well with those therapists who are available.

In psychoanalytic literature we can find a great number of examples showing how different and individually conditioned evaluations are. With a year's interval two American psychoanalysts had the same immortal patient in analysis: Sophocles' Antigone. The striking difference in their interpretations should probably be seen in connection with the distinctions in their temperament and life experience.

Philip Weissman considers Antigone a pre-Oedipally fixated old maid and emphasizes her passive features: she is inspired by a need to take things gently but irrefutably in her own hands and is prepared to destroy herself at this task. He believes that today we can find the character of Antigone in the "various roles of a lifelong dedicated personal aide to either a famous man or woman, and to the respective families."[26]

Benjamin Wolman, on the contrary, focuses on Antigone's active characteristics. Antigone is high-spirited and unwilling to compromise. She will not submit to lawless, arbitrary forces. He compares her to the people of the resistance movement during the Second World War and the warriors in the Israeli War of Independence: "Antigone ate and drank, and hoped some day to be happily married to Hamon. . . . She loved to live, but her vectoral love for justice was stronger than the love for herself."[27]

As far as I can see, there is nothing else for the modern-day Miss Antigone to do but find her therapist on her own if she wants to solve her not inconsiderable human problems.

It is also important for the person in charge of referring patients not to "send" them to a therapist but instead to "advise" them to visit the therapist concerned and not to be offended if the patient comes back and asks to be directed to someone else. A patient who has the freedom to choose his therapist for himself is also more willing to take responsibility for his treatment, and it is easier for him to develop a spontaneous and personal feeling of confidence. The thought that "I've been sent for treatment" can fixate an alienated outlook and prevent a personal, spontaneous relationship with the therapist—and without this there can be no improvement—from developing. Finally, the interpersonal relationship will then also determine the geographical distance the patient has to walk, quite irrespective of parking lots, bus routes and possibly subway stations.

For the psychoanalyst the initial sessions with a new patient can be a fascinating encounter. In front of one's surprised gaze a whole new world opens up with immediate clarity and convincing authenticity. "The innocent freshness of first sight" that Stephen Spender talks about is reserved not only for artists. It is like a source of all creative activity—among others, the psychoanalyst's—which it also sets in motion. The first encounter leaves a permanent impression. What the patient communicates—or demonstratively neglects to communicate— may not become ripe enough for psychoanalytic observation until much later, in the final phase of treatment. My feeling is that you can trust this first, intuitive sense of the whole. It is durable and seldom misleading. But there we also find lurking in new disguise the stubborn old illusion of natural human closeness: the faith that I know who the person sitting across from me really is. This absolute interpretation of mine was modified when I worked together with a psychiatrist who knows exceptionally well how people and their idiosyncrasies function within the inscrutable and complicated machinery of society, and with a Rorschach diagnostician who has succeeded in finding a functional connection between structural conflicts and characteristic manifest behavior. New perspectives appeared, and my total view of a patient was related to the different frame of reference other people had. My view of a patient as a whole proved to be totally relevant within the framework of psychoanalysis but relative outside it: it was one view among many.

The insight that the genuine understanding of the whole picture is relative in itself need not be frustrating. On the contrary, the change in perspective may enrich the original idea. In a pluralistic society the diagnosis should also be pluralistic, for the benefit of the patient and the person caring for him. "Man," wrote Karl Jaspers, "differs from everything else in the world in that it is equally impossible for him as a whole to become an object as it is for the world as a whole. When he is recognized, it is something in his being that is recognized, not he himself."[28] Not only in the psychoanalyst's office did the alienated human being report his existence. The rootless stranger without any identity entered literature as well as social and political controversies. Everywhere he is represented as victim—victim of unsympathetic society, of godlessness, of the relativity of values and of working conditions under industrial capitalism. In no sense do I wish to deny that all these factors make it difficult for modern man to find an orientation in life. But when has there existed a society that made it easy for people to live in it? I wonder if the alienated human being is a victim of our democratic society or if it isn't rather the other way around. He may get along pretty well in an authoritarian society, but the grounds of his being crumble when he moves in a society in which he is endlessly expected to express his likes and dislikes, to make choices and take on responsibilities.

When we view the existence of alienated people from the outside it seems like an exceptionally good way of avoiding conflicts—especially with authorities. A servant who expressed a certain opinion was in danger of losing his job and so was a manual laborer with political views—not merely with several months' notice but on the spot. Children who obeyed without grumbling, women who acquiesced without objections to having their husbands run the family's life hardly had an opportunity to know what they themselves wanted or to develop a vision of their own. Their identity was left up to the father of the family and could be quite peculiar and even plainly asocial. Sometimes psychopathological reactions may also tell us something about the conditions people of former generations lived under.

In many cases today it is completely impossible to understand the gulf that separated ordinary people from the "powers above." The historian Friedrich Heer writes about a petition the peasants in Würtemberg—in the time of Schiller—sent to the overlord. It says, "The landed proprietor's swine [which in the petition seem to have a much higher rank and greater dignity than the peasants] have badly ravaged the fields and brought to the verge of desperation his most humble and obedient peasants, who had no rights to take measures against these subjects of the landlord."[29] Complaints like this are typical of the lot of the European peasant population from the twelfth to the nineteenth century.[30] What kind of an identity could such a peasant have had? At least not of being the crowning glory of creation. The king's swine were several notches above them. A special quality must have been lacking in their sense of identity: the feeling of an existential humanity in relation to animals. When we also add that the remains of skeletons from the middle ages have revealed a high rate of infant mortality and a state of chronic malnutrition (which can only be compared with that of present-day India) among the peasant population, then there must have been scarcely any sign of a sense of identity among the people. "Here we catch a glimpse," says Heer, "of a great tragedy that permeated the existence of the peasant population: the very people whose work secured the supply of provisions often did not have enough bread and milk for themselves and their children."[31]

Constant alienation as a form of human life does not—psychologically speaking—make its first appearance with the onset of industrialism; it seems to have existed and been accepted for centuries. In a society in which all the rules and regulations were made unconditionally by the landowners and the church fathers (*cuius regio—eius religio* [whoever governs the region controls the religion]), alienation was probably an authentic form of life. The need for change could appear only when the structure of society was such that each citizen was able to assert his influence, either by voting for one of several political parties or through membership in a trade organization which represented his professional interests in relation to the state and his employer.

It seems to me that the public debate confirms the alienated person's expectations that external forces—society and its institutions—provide him with his sense of meaning. The alienated person hardly ever suffers from depression. At the beginning of a continuum the depressive person stands reproaching himself, whereas the alienated person with his demands on the outer world stands at the end. "Depressive people assign the meaning of their lives to factors within themselves, the alienated to factors outside themselves," says Frieda Fromm-Reichmann.[32] The depressive person is primarily interested in attaining something in this world, while the alienated person is occupied with the question of whether "life" has treated him badly or well and registering his answer. The depressive reaction seems to be a natural part of a dynamic democracy. The alienated sense of life reflects the feeling of man's helplessness in relation to an authoritarian government whose decisions cannot be questioned with a "Why?" or a "Where does that lead to?"

When an alienated person today seeks treatment from a

therapist, it is a promising sign that he is beginning to rebel against his formless existence and vague identity. I find it extremely positive that anonymous people—who are indifferent and apathetic—tire of their alienation and announce their desire to change and their right to receive help in their efforts to do so.

"Many people are compelled to live without contempt and without esteem for themselves or their lives, because need forces them so close to life that they do not have any peace or quiet to describe themselves and name their conditions,"[33] writes Lars Gyllensten.

But perhaps we are heading for a time when we will be able to talk about this in the past tense.

Throughout this essay I have used the term "alienation" in its clinical, diagnostic sense quite apart from the classical concept of alienation presented by Marx, who in turn got it from Feuerbach. It is hard to know whether the clinical term, which was first used in the United States, was consciously adopted from Marx, but this does not seem unlikely. Marx's concept of alienation includes the comprehensive philosophical system of historical materialism and uses some psychological observations that may be interesting to examine briefly. Alienation has acquired a renewed relevance in our own highly industrialized mass society, in which the latent feeling of human estrangement has become manifest and stands out as a complicated political, social and psychological problem of explosive power.

Marx claimed that inhuman working conditions and a general state of inequity deprived industrial workers of their identity and made them into lifeless objects and commodities. "The more a laborer works, the more powerful becomes the world of the alien objects he is creating while he himself and his inner world get poorer—and belong less to him." Only through a changed structure of work and common ownership of the means of production will the debased and alienated laborer be able to win back his identity and recover his dignity as a human being.

He believed that man's dignity and his identity are due to the fact that as a unique being he has existential freedom. "Man," so Marx claimed, "relates to himself as a universal and therefore a free being."[34] When we think of Friedrich Heer's description of the peasant population during the middle ages the people seem to have lived under the same kind of conditions as the working class in Marx's time. On the basis of the psychological knowledge available today, I would rather say that degrading social conditions and chronic malnutrition can prevent large segments of the population from developing an awareness of their individuality. Presumably they lived in a state of primary alienation, apathy and indifference and were unable to take care of themselves. They knew nothing about freedom. They were not deprived of an identity. They had none. Identity is a product of culture. It is not inborn.

Today the blacks are in the same predicament as the peasants and industrial workers were in earlier times. But James Baldwin, who speaks in their cause, has gained a deeper insight: "The world has not left a place for you and, if the world had its way, such a place would never exist." He believes that the blacks see this truth quite nakedly. But the whites are still waiting to get their identity for nothing.

> So the anguish that can seize a white man makes itself felt in the middle of his life. Then with an almost incomprehensible effort he has to give up everything he has ever expected or believed. Then he has to leave this world and go out into the void, or what seems like the void.[35]

In terms of my clinical experience, Baldwin's observations are correct. Among the people who seek psychoanalytic treatment today there is a distinct group between the ages of forty and fifty who are caught in a crisis. They have often achieved a good social position and their family relations are good. But an incomprehensible anxiety has seized them. They've begun to realize that they've been waiting for something that doesn't seem to be turning up. No big, glittering fairy-tale bird is about to whisper a secret into their ear—as in Miró's painting,

"A beautiful bird revealing the Unknown to a pair of lovers." They are beginning to realize that they themselves must figure out the secret of their existence.

But even if Baldwin's point of view fits in better with the clinical experience of our day, it also gives a frightening picture of the crisis of trust that large groups of the population are going through today. The feeling of being welcome in the world can certainly lead to unforgivable passivity and, objectively speaking, is not enduring. But the subjective feeling that "the whole world welcomes you" determines a child's attitude to his environment in relation to his faith in others and in himself. The deterioration in the human climate becomes evident when, for example, we compare Baldwin's statement with an autobiographical reflection by Freud.[36] Even though as a Jew he was denied a place in his own country, he was convinced that somewhere in the world there would indeed always be a small place for him, where he could be of use. As we know, he was of use in London during the last year of his life.

Marx had a dualistic concept of man's existence that seems surprisingly modern. Man, he said, is equipped with natural powers of life, drives, expressed in his will to work toward a goal and his pleasure in creating. He differs from animals in his capacity to reflect over his own actions. He is also a "suffering being" because he is aware of his own imperfections and his limitations. The feeling of inadequacy is the necessary incitement to further development, to an endless creative activity. Consequently, man is both an active, creative being directed outward and a passive, suffering being directed inward.[37]

Work is the function of human beings, determined by the species, and has a central place in their psychological model. Animals can only produce under the pressure of immediate biological needs. But man produces irrespective of them and basically "in freedom" from these needs.

"This production is the effective means of his innate life. Through it nature comes to be his value and his reality." Expressed in more modern terms, we can say that work forms man's consciousness: of his inherent capacity and of the structure in his environment. According to this, work is both identity and interpretation.

Nature and its wealth—that is to say, the nonhuman environment—become conscious factors in our lives only when they are realized through human work. Goal-oriented activity creates social ties that unite people with each other. Work serves to form the primary human contact. The young Marx writes in praise of work:

> When you enjoy or use my product I will immediately recognize my own enjoyment in my awareness of having satisfied some human needs through my work and also because I have brought to light the human essence and thus satisfied the need of another human essence for this object. By means of work, I know I am acknowledged both in your thoughts and in your love.

Man's dignity is his meaningful conscious activity. It makes him fit into human society. For Marx, alienation is a state of degradation, a "perversion," that occurs when man is stripped of his dignity and his characteristic freedom by having his work reified, which makes it exist outside him and isolates him from mutual contact. But later on Marx says that the ruling class also lives in a state of *Selbstentfremdung* [alienation from self], but it relishes its alienation as a sign of its social power in society—a somewhat peculiar contention, more spiteful than psychologically convincing. To live in a state of alienation from oneself doesn't make anybody happy.

In Arnold Ljungdal,[38] who is one of the leading advocates of Marxism—and also of psychoanalysis—in the Nordic countries, the rage has given way to a universal human vision of an insoluble tragic conflict in which neither the master nor the servant has any choice. Both are compelled to function in a system that forces them inexorably into alienation. They are alienated from themselves and strangers to each other.

We may ask ourselves if society will ever be organized in such a way that human alienation, the existential aloneness, can be completely overcome. For the benefit of the whole, no doubt we must all allow for a certain depersonalized area in our lives. Man is, as Marx said, an imperfect, suffering being.

Marx believed that his concept of man was a primary model. I rather tend to believe that this model holds true for man in Western civilization, in which his active, creative needs were affirmed and promoted.[39] This attitude was the prerequisite for the development of Western technology and also for the formation of a special superego structure in the demand for autonomy, responsibility and veracity. Marx's idea that man has an ability to look at his work critically and with perspective calls for a rather advanced society, a society that permits a certain freedom of choice: I can do this or that or I can refrain from doing anything. If a child can develop such selective attitudes, he must feel relatively secure. Protected against starvation. Protected from being forced to act according to prescribed standards. Protected inasmuch as his parents appreciate, to a certain degree at least, the child's efforts to be autonomous and independent.

That which was a self-evident prerequisite for Marx, and to a certain degree also for Freud, is not self-evident to James Baldwin. He has probably seen too many children who do not live under such circumstances. But through his contempt for the innocent dream of white men we can also hear, if I'm not mistaken, a tone of envy. "It is terrible to say so, but for a very long time the problems of white people seemed to me to be unreal. They made me think of babies who cry when they can't have the breast."

Is it possible that the outcast is envious of the white man's secure childhood, which carries memories of warmth and color that we have otherwise never experienced? When people sang "The International" while the ground was still bare in the misty spring, surely at that moment there were many who were completely convinced that the sun would never set again on the world of tomorrow. *"Da scheint die Sonne ohne Unterlass."* (Here the sun shines forever.)

The search for the heavenly city, the dream of building a

civitas dei, a kingdom of God here on earth, is a constantly recurring theme in our Western culture. Everyone can choose freely among the many different interpretations. The vision of a classless society was Marx's contribution, and he devoted all his creative energies to it.

And Freud is not missing from the company of utopians. He bases his theory of primary narcissism on the fact that a newborn child experiences a brief state of bliss, happily immersed in itself and completely independent of its environment: an autonomous world within the world. This short phase of primary harmony and gentle relaxation is the archetype of man's lost paradise, which he will always long for. It becomes a prototype for all experiences of happiness in later life. Freud describes a state that for many people seems self-evident. But in the formulation of his theory, he identified with the child's glorious denial of his utterly helpless state. Primary narcissism is not primary. It is completely dependent on an indulgent, caring object, on the mother's intuitive sensitivity to the child's needs and her ability to satisfy them without disturbing the child's balance. H. Kohut has presented a cautious and needful interpretation of Freud's theory. He says that primary narcissism "contains the assumption that the child originally perceives the mother and her caretaking not as a 'thou' and its activities but within the framework of a viewpoint in which the I-thou distinction has not yet been established. Therefore the expected control over the mother and her caretaking is closer to the image an adult has of himself and of the control he himself expects to have over his own body and soul than the way an adult experiences others and his control over them."[40]

Freud believed that everybody knows what happiness is because everyone has experienced it at the beginning of his life. Equipped with the same expectations, my encounters with alienated patients became a deeply moving experience. Many of them had no clear idea of what happiness was. Nor did they know how it felt to be happy, unreservedly happy through and through. It was as difficult to talk about happiness with an alienated patient as it is to explain to a blind child what a fairy is.[41]

The fact that I stubbornly keep returning to the assumption that the sense of identity is an acquired trait is a consequence not of the psychological expert's pedantry or dissatisfaction, but of a growing concern over the fact that man's inherent psychic equipment is overestimated while his need for maturation and integration is underestimated. An unrealistic view of man's qualifications can mobilize inadequate reactions—not to say unfounded disappointment—that may have serious social and political consequences.

The vital source of inspiration for all movements of social reform has been the image of the naturally rich, harmonious and free human being who will appear in all his perfection when the bonds of social oppression and social injustice have fallen. People have fought faithfully and tenaciously for the man born free in nature. But today that idea has become a source of disappointment—sometimes bordering on misanthropy. After generations of struggle and strife, people achieved unprecedented security and freedom, and yet not a trace of the beautiful images of the Greek gods—which for decades have embellished the covers of progressive books and journals—was realized. The new man did not spring forth perfect and ready-made, like Pallas Athena out of Zeus' head. On the contrary, he often behaves in a quite infantile and unreasonable manner. Nor was he always attractive to look at—and neither was a search for a uniform style his strength. Nor do we find many signs of gratitude for the new freedom and the good life he has received. But despite everything, a person must keep his spirits up if he is willing to review his own concepts and abandon misleading wishful thinking. Instead, perhaps we can try to imagine what it feels like to emerge from the blind cellar existence of alienation into the dazzling light of day. We don't know how many, overwhelmed by loneliness and confusion, turn back to the darkness.

The impatience and bitterness resulting from unfulfilled expectations may produce dangerous short circuits that lead to a new form of tutelage and a quiet new scorn for the masses, not least within the radical movement that supported this development.

I believe that modern psychoanalysis can help prevent such affect-conditioned reactions. Not by counseling—there is far too much of that nowadays, and the phrase "it's easier said than done" is a commonplace—but by advancing a more realistic view of man's development. Instead of waiting for inherent characteristics to appear, we should insist that man's incredible ability to learn and reevaluate, his tendency even in old age to find new solutions endlessly to old conflicts, can give cause for cautious optimism. Many of his reactions that may seem negative or downright pathological may be an effort to adjust himself to a new situation, a new environment. The future of psychoanalysis in today's society lies with the communication of this realization: to support human endurance in extended and demanding conflict situations and to prevent catastrophic, irrational reactions.

From this angle I cannot help but have some reservations about certain tendencies in modern education. It tends to underestimate the child's vital efforts toward psychic development by means of learning, identification (which is also a learning process) and the acquisition of knowledge. We can prevent a child from developing the largest and most subtle vocabulary possible by dismissing his questions and interests on the grounds that they're too advanced for his age. They seem to lie beyond the child's present phase of development. Instead, we believe that the child matures of his own accord with or without the least possible incentive from outside. After overcoming a state of physiological malnutrition, we seem to be heading for a psychic one instead.

In a brief short story called "Growing"[42] the novelist Pär Rådström writes about seven-year-old Pumpen, who can't start school with his friends but has to wait another year. He has described his feeling of loneliness, bitterness and distrust toward the adults who don't understand how much he wants to start right away. In the solitude of the deserted parks, he meets a grown-up man with whom he can share his sorrow. "Do you want some ice cream?" the man asks to console him. Suddenly Pumpen starts to hate this unsuspecting nice gentleman.

"He's just like Mom and Dad. If there is something you really want very much, you can never have it, you get ice cream instead, or you get to go to the movies, or you get a big piece of chocolate or a car. . . .

"If you didn't get what you wanted, at least you could still have that. At least you could do without it. Not try to trick what you wanted to have by forgetting it. Pumpen didn't want any ice cream because he knew it tasted good and then suddenly while licking the ice cream you would forget that you wanted to go to school. And that was treason. It was betraying everything."

After a while, resigned, Pumpen went along to the ice-cream stand.

Pumpen will be waiting another year, a very long year. Pumpen cannot bear to think about it. He decides that it is best to stop thinking and to stop asking people questions.

"Here I sit waiting," he thought. "If I sit here and wait, and never ask what time it is, it may go faster."

Freud believed that when a person is forbidden to think or ask questions, this may cause a suppression of conflicts and lead to a neurotic development.

Is it possible that we have very quietly acquired new masters? Relying on various scientific studies, adults divide up the portions of psychic growth. Not too much, my little friend, and not too little either! Could it be that Pumpen is the David Copperfield of our age?

Modern education deprives the child of his dignity and underestimates his strength by providing him with a tension-less, static concept of life as secure, simple and dispassionate, according to Lionel Trilling, writing about American conditions in *Commentary*.

In the foregoing I have tried to sketch a picture of the way in which the crisis of trust in interpersonal relations has forced its way into the psychoanalyst's office and brought about a re-orientation in the concepts of psychoanalytic theories. There is another side to this crisis of trust that the psychoanalyst cannot ignore: the problematic relation modern man has to the nonhuman environment,[43] his disorientation in the technologized metropolitan environment, which directly influences his relationships with other people and dehumanizes them.

If someone asked me what neurotic symptom was typical of our time, I would reply without hesitation: phobia.

Conversion hysteria was the classic symptom of Freud's day. Anna O., Breuer's and Freud's first patient, loved her father in a way unbefitting a daughter. She rejected her love and had to deal instead with a paralyzed arm: a compromise between suppressed desire, loyalty to her father, and no small degree of aggressiveness toward her mother. Everything points to the fact that her inner world was governed by passionate, intensive human relations. It seems that she did not have any identity problems.

The symptom of conversion is a result of conflicts in interpersonal relationships. In the symptom of phobia a third party has directly or indirectly announced its presence: the nonhuman environment. In phobia the threat of losing one's identity is more acute than with the chronically alienated. But even the alienated person, who has reduced himself to an object, a robot, is guided from the outside by undefinable forces, experiences some sort of identity in his existence as a thing. In the symptom of phobia the identity crisis has progressed one step further. Even the "identity of an object," which still includes an awareness of substance and limits, has disappeared.

In an attack of phobia, as described by adult patients, the individual has temporarily lost control over his cognitive functions. The patient feels paralyzed and disoriented. His sense of orientation falters or is turned off completely. His vision becomes unclear. The outlines of a room disintegrate and collapse. The surrounding space is either frighteningly empty or filled with soaring, chaotic forms of unrecognizable character. Familiar sounds can no longer be localized and they may rise to a terrible shrill pitch, or they may disappear completely and the silence may become equated with deafness. The sense of the body's continuity is reduced, which creates a feeling that the limbs are only loosely joined together and are gradually being exhausted, drained of all muscular strength. The whole body seems to lose weight and could easily be swept away by the faintest breath of wind. Patients are unable to stand upright and they feel an intense need to lie down flat on the ground—perhaps the only mechanism of flight still remaining in the state of utter powerlessness in the face of an overwhelming, undefinable danger.

But despite the anguish, the phobic attack is experienced not only in a negative way. On the contrary, it is often accompanied by a peculiar fluctuation between fascination and aversion. The patient approaches it with an apparently cheerful sense of expectation that suddenly turns into an incomprehensible terror and an unsuccessful attempt to flee.

The most conspicuous trait in the picture of phobia is the absence of people. They have left no traces and nothing suggests their previous or present existence. The phobic vacuum gives a sense of terror-struck, traumatic isolation.

In my experience the emotional basis of phobia seems to be an extremely dramatic and very early crisis of confidence in which both people and the environment first invited the child to approach and then betrayed him. Innocence and trust are transformed into feelings of rage and confusion that gradually give way to a sense of loneliness and shame. A feeling of being totally abandoned and having lost all expectations of trust is a universal human experience and can occur in any age group.

Hardly anyone's childhood goes by without passing phobic reactions. In adults we can often observe remnants of phobic states of anguish: a tendency to get tired in company, slight feelings of dizziness on streets with heavy traffic or in empty open spaces or a general inability to bear changes in the balance of activity and passivity—that is to say, under stress. A healthy adult recovers quickly from these slight feelings of disintegration and discovers the remedy spontaneously: the incomparable integrating power of sleep. Fully developed symptoms of phobia even appear during convalescence from an illness and disappear when the person is fully recovered. In old age phobic reactions tend to be more serious and noticeable. Quite naturally, because of diminished mobility and weakened sense preceptions, the orientation to the nonhuman environment is made more difficult. Social isolation and the diminished contact with people of one's own generation add to a tragic sense of final, incurable loneliness. This often leads to the development of a phobic personality among old people, who often react with hostility, disorientation and fright to stimuli from the outside world and who are sometimes erroneously accused of being paranoid.

The motivation of phobia works on two levels. First it appears on a primitive, unstructured level of development, but a little later it is reactivated on a relatively high level of integration. The school phobias young people experience show that they cannot accept their father's normative authority. But when they haven't been able to accept inner limitations, they will soon draw the lines outside themselves, in their external surroundings. It soon becomes apparent how insecure and confusing it is to live in an environment, an external world, structured by limits that should actually exist within the individual himself.

On the primitive level the phobias of infants reveal a fundamental crisis in confidence and confusion of aggressive feelings. The child cannot localize the source of aggressiveness and is incapable of drawing the line between aggressiveness that comes from within and that which others direct toward him from the outside. One of the earliest disturbances in the development of an identity occurs here. All identity requires a perception of the continuity of one's own body and its boundaries in the environment. Along with the cognitive functions, it is primarily the kinesthetic sense that is the matrix of development.

I think it is misleading to describe phobia—as some authorities have done—as an "anxiety about anxiety." In the early crisis of trust in which phobia has its roots the process of differentiation between child and parents is not quite complete, and the child doesn't yet have any lasting image of its parents.

When the parents are not present—even if only for a short while—the child also loses the awareness of his own existence. The mother of a young patient who suffered from phobia described it very simply: "Everything is fine, as long as she's with us, but as soon as she's alone it gets to her." "It" was a phobic sense of emptiness and terror with which the young woman, who otherwise was talented and socially well adapted, had struggled since her childhood.

In many instances the nonhuman environment can offer some protection against phobic attack and should not be underestimated even though the scope may be limited. R. D. Laing describes a woman who felt free of her phobia as long as she stayed in her parents' apartment, but when she went out the noise and the anonymity of the street broke the magic setting of her home.

It seems to me that phobic reactions occur not only because of a crisis in trust in interpersonal relations but also in relation to the nonhuman environment. In our age perhaps one of the great difficulties of adaptability, especially for small children and old people, is in the inadequate sense of belonging to the mechanized surroundings of a big city. The big-city environment—in general an environment dominated by the technology —does not seem to convey directly a sense of security. A surplus of stimuli that cannot be immediately placed, experiences of sudden changes in speed and of the displacement of one's own body in space, and consequently the ensuing changes in the kinesthetic sense of body image, predisposes people to phobic reactions.

One patient who suffered from street phobia had grown up in a densely populated area that was especially inhospitable to children. The members of the family had to shout to each other when they wanted to be heard. The street below broadcast an endless current of whirring, groaning, explosive sounds. Only for a few hours at night was it quiet. He would wake up to the silence of the night—it made him feel free and at ease, but also left him with a feeling of indescribable anguish at the emptiness. He was afraid of resting, of having everything around him quiet.

But he was also deeply fascinated by the silence. He dreamed of life in the country in harmony with nature's organic rhythm. During the course of the analysis he started to protect himself from his restlessness, which sometimes approached chaos, and his inability to be on time and keep appointments. But he felt that these attitudes were not part of an inner conflict or immaturity, but a conflict with a traumatizing environment. "I guess I have to be more careful. Not always plunge right in. In a detective story by Dorothy Sayers, a man was killed because he was sitting too close to the church bells. In five minutes he was dead. From sitting near some eight or ten bells when they were ringing all at once. A person can die from noise! I must have a hard time apportioning things!" I've often remembered his words. I know of no better antinoise propaganda.

This patient suffered from a considerable disturbance in his body image. Particularly in the beginning of the treatment, he slipped back several times into primitive body sensations. They were probably provoked by the forced physical passivity that the analytic situation imposes and that prevented him from acting out his anguish and discomfort through muscular activity. He lay very still; he felt he was absent and strangely light. His hand and his upper and lower arm swayed lightly, each on their own, above his body. His feet and legs seemed to be headed toward the back wall of the room. His voice was thin and had a dreamlike, childishly wondrous sound.

After having one of these experiences, he came back the following day, pale and with his eyes deeply set. He held himself convulsively to conceal his trembling. Instead of greeting me, he stood motionless, mumbling: "It's not going to work, it's not going to work." On his way home from the previous session, he had suddenly felt as if the street were slowly rising up at him. He couldn't defend himself. It rose higher and higher and threatened to strike him. Or he was about to fall into it. He couldn't decide which. He tried to walk very slowly, step by step, with his eyes fixed on each individual piece of asphalt. And he started to count them.

In a short story called *"En bas vers la mort"* ("Deep Down

Toward Death")[44] Jean Marie le Clézio describes the panic-stricken reaction of a man called Mallansèmes during an automobile ride. He is losing control over his body's continuity at a speed that races the growing speed of the car, while his vision becomes more and more blurred. The constantly rising crescendo of the drive ends in a dramatic loss of identity:

> Now he passed the last house in the city at eighty kilometers per hour. He caught glimpses of open doors, garage exits, workers in blue, immobile next to their thundering machines, lost in the spots of asphalt, patches of tar and steam shooting past, and farther away where the highway cut straight as an arrow through the landscape like a flowing gray tone, a frontier river dividing continents of moorland and thickets. In the front seat of the car, Mallansèmes was still present, visibly devouring the wild fury of the speeding car. The speedometer showed 120 k.m.h. but that was a faint indication compared with what could be seen on his smoke-colored glasses. This straight line was engraved on his brain, in his throat, along his spine, all the way down to his Achilles tendons. It made his body stiffen in a spasm that was both conscious and physical. . . .
>
> And his hand. Mallansèmes' left hand has pushed against the steering wheel. With all its might. But only his hand. Since the rest of the body's already someplace else, perhaps impaled on top of that new telephone pole, perhaps floating in the bowels of the earth, anchored at the roots of a tree. . . .
>
> He smiled a last smile before he felt himself grow so small, so small that no one would ever find him again.

People are drawn into the urban environment and reduced to nonhuman forms without a face of their own or any special characteristics.

Tord Bäckström, the art critic of a Gothenburg newspaper, has written about a film that describes the loss of personal relationships among people who live in high-rise buildings and the lack of selectivity in a collective housing environment. After a long day at work, the husband drives home in his car. He looks up at the high-rise where he lives to see if his wife is standing at the window waving to him. But when he looks up at the building, there are many women standing waving to him. Which one is the woman who is waiting for him and nobody else? He doesn't know. A child who is playing in the sandbox suddenly has an idea and calls up to his mother. When he looks at the facade of the building, countless windows open up and countless women call for the child. But which woman did the child call for? Which one is his own mother who gives him the security that this child alone wants?

In a desolate wilderness, when a person cries for help and neither God nor man hears him, a dramatic, universal situation occurs in condensed form and conveys a sense of utter loneliness and despair.

In an overpopulated metropolis, when a person cries for help, and far away, at a distance, sees something move that could be a human being but whose movements have no meaning for him, a senseless, phobia-like situation takes place and a feeling of unreality and alienation is conveyed.

When K.[45] is about to be executed in a quarry outside the city, he remains silent. But his eyes look for the people of the city—as a last hope of human intimacy and perhaps also of help:

> His glance fell on the top story of the house adjoining the quarry. Like candlelight it flared up, the casements of a window there suddenly flew open; a human figure, faint and insubstantial at that distance and that height, leaned abruptly far forward and stretched both arms still farther. Who was it? A friend? A good man? Someone who sympathized? Someone who wanted to help? Was it one person only? Or was it mankind? Was help at hand?[46]

In *Var Lösen* (*Our Watchword*) Asta Bolin discusses the "faceless" society in which "all doors are like those of a closed institution with only a number plate marking a difference," and points out the phobic reaction lurking in the overpopulated technological environment, the feeling of the big city's unlimited freedom: "All doors are open" can suddenly turn into a claustrophobic sense of terror: "All doors are closed!" And who knows if there's anybody behind them?

Near where I live there is an exemplary little park with an abundance of lovely roses, a lawn, a fountain, a wading pond à la Luxembourg, swings and a free Ping-Pong table, and a lady to look after children from noon to seven o'clock. The children who play there are well behaved, well fed and well dressed. Sometimes they call on me for one thing or another. They want you to give them 50 öre to buy ice cream, to accompany them to a certain street, to tell them what time it is or to conduct a short "adult" conversation with them. About the weather and the world: "Don't you think it's a little too hot this summer, Ma'm?" All this spontaneous trust might make me feel very happy and flattered. But it doesn't. The children never recognize me. They look at me every time in the same unchanging, matter-of-fact, somewhat surprised way. I am incidental and will remain that way. And there are so many random events in the park.

Children who grow up in small towns or in the country meet considerably fewer people than urban children. They recognize them when they meet them in their daily life, on their way to school or to play in the park. Whereas children in big cities meet almost exclusively an indeterminate number of anonymous people and often see them from a special urban perspective, whether from high above or underground in a continuous flow. In raising children we probably should emphasize particularly the child's ability to make choices and to have a highly developed sense of quality. This is the prerequisite for feeling that you yourself and your neighbor are individual and unique beings.

In densely populated areas, apparently, intense and profound human relations don't seem to sprout up of their own accord.

It seems to me that the crisis of trust is also one of the dominating factors in modern art. Concrete, structural art tangibly reminds the viewer of the ways in which the nonhuman environment breaks down habitual patterns of perception. At the same time completely new configurations—which must be learned—have appeared in the fields of science and technology.

The contact of the eye with the object is often indirect, transmitted through an instrument, an alienated eye. In this way Sigurd Persson, for example, in his early enamel works used irregular clusters of one-celled organisms—seen under a microscope—as an ornament against a dark background. Or to take another extreme: Lars Eklund[47] has brought a very remote cirrus cloud into immediate visual proximity. For the first time in a reconstruction, executed with great precision, the human eye can see its wonderful light rhythm and its floating blue range of color.

The numerous paintings of white on white demand a more subtle and discerning vision, a great sensitivity to optical impressions. In its chaste geometric precision the perforated surface of Lucio Fontana's paintings convey a sense of space in a nascent state. Pierre Rouvé[48] believes that this primal state must be measured by heartbeats, not cubic inches—a poetic way of illustrating the unique feeling in Fontana's work that the boundary between outer and inner space has been abolished, especially by the lightness of the white color and its boundless presence. In a painting by Malevich[49] the almost indiscernible transition between two colors—a wide white cross on gray— demands a highly developed ability to differentiate between optical impressions.

We find it also striking that a work of modern art induces a breakdown in customary optical configurations and consciously strives for a new configuration. It is difficult to say whether the work of art sets the viewer in motion or whether the viewer's movements create the art work. I am thinking of the huge, flickering walls—mainly in the Stedelijk Museum in Amsterdam —where constantly changing optical configurations glide back and forth in accord with the visitor's own movements. The walls evoke a feeling of visual and kinetic disorientation because one no longer perceives as fixed the relation of one's body to the room —it changes constantly.

I believe that much of the stress in a large city is caused by an inability to combine the various stimuli to which people are exposed into a general pattern of perception of the character of signs. Our secure, relatively static everyday logic—in which *a* is *a* and not *b*—is more of a hindrance than a help. The fact that two opposites can form the impression of a whole and at the same time maintain their identity can be a revolutionary discovery, at least for older people, whose perceptions are affected by a less dynamic environment. In a relief Lars Englund[50] has united the hollow space and the elbow room of a large city in a homogeneous configuration in which concave and convex remain what they are but at the same time form a harmoniously balanced whole, an endless continuity of itself.

It may also be germane to consider here a renewed awareness of all the big and little objects that so imperceptibly form part of our daily life—from Kurt Schwitter's masculine, rigorously logical collages made of matchboxes, newspapers and small pennies to the graceful play of used waxed paper, chocolate wrappers and other oddments by Madeleine Pyk, or the sick, swollen objects from everyday life by Claus Oldenburg, reminding the viewer that even objects can be neglected and left to die slowly.

The new interest in unfamiliar optical configurations and their relationship to space may often seem shocking to the viewer and may even evoke anxiety and dizziness. But this encounter may also contribute to making him feel less alienated in a human environment fundamentally changed. "Art tells us about the evolution of our visual knowledge," says Charles Biederman.[51] As a viewer I find in this art that reshapes perceptions—which is so wonderfully free from the one-sided moralizing of social realism—a clearly pedagogical point of view. Look closely! Let yourself be surprised! Re-learn!

But the emotional appeal also remains. It is in the things themselves, in their structure.

Paul Klee once said that art need not portray what is visible, but instead it must make that which is invisible visible for everyone.

As a transition to a more painterly attitude I scratch my picture with a blackened piece of glass. A playful experiment on a porcelain plate gave me the idea. So the medium is no longer a black line but a white one. White energy on a nocturnal background, and the words "Let there be light!" perfectly executed. And so I glide softly into the new world of nuances.[52]

But what has become of his adventurous young lady with a mousy face? She waved a cheerful farewell as she briskly and lightly tripped along, into the fairy-tale forest. She doesn't seem to have come out.

The human figure as a whole has disappeared. It has been absorbed by things. Man is reduced to a quality in the non-human environment. Man has become a structure.

"Houses," Utrillo wrote in 1923, "have a soul in their secret depths." He was also the first person to convey something of the big city's desolation. His tragic life made him sensitive to the alienation that modern man was to experience in it.

Utrillo (1883–1955) was the illegitimate child of a famous mother. When he was born, she worked as a model for Monet, among others, and her name was Marie Clementine Coulon. When she changed her profession and became a painter, she called herself Suzanne Valadon. When the boy was around five or six years old, she married and became Madame Moussis. After a while she was divorced and soon became Madame Utter.

Utrillo never found out who his father was. He had a choice of two French painters—Puvis de Chavannes and Voissis—and a Spanish journalist, Miguel Utrillo, who became his official father and gave him his name. He pitied the little boy and adopted him, but never acknowledged him as his own son.

When Utrillo was thirty-five years old, an American widow, Mrs. Lucy Pauwels, saved him from alcoholism and insanity, against his will, and also married him. She became a painter and called herself Lucy Valore with reference to her mother-in-law.

There were no rules in Utrillo's upbringing and none at all in his later life, during which time he was fighting constantly with the police and other authorities until his wife brought him external order, social stability and artistic stagnation. His most important artistic work was produced between the ages of nineteen and twenty-nine, when he was in and out of insane asylums. That was his famous "white period."

Utrillo is called "the painter in whites." He often mixed plaster of Paris and liquid cement with his white paint to give it an uneven surface. Nearly everything is white: the facades of houses, the streets, but above all the walls. He painted the walls the way they were, or rather the way they had been built, and sometimes they look "dirty and uneven like crumbled plaster . . . sometimes they seem to have been put together by a mason's trowel."[53] His white snow vibrates, changes tones and has the quality of human skin. But walls are also boundaries—limits in the exterior space. Utrillo painted them white—white as the walls in Montmartre, white as the Holy Virgin and her son, whom he loved and worshipped. It was a big step from the cool, white Mary to the passionate, dark Suzanne. It reveals something of the child's ability to re-create reality, even though the ambivalence remained. The white is never absolutely pure, and sometimes it speaks of disintegration, pollution and decay. But the white wall may also represent a memory of the fact that the mother was the first environment the child had and her body the first boundary he encountered. The striking tactile quality of the walls may suggest the fact that the first demarcation occurs through touch and, at that stage, sight is less significant.

There are people who unconsciously go on living in this undifferentiated state, which is a source of chronic anguish and disorientation. Bengt Nerman has grasped the inherent logic of alienation that borders on the psychotic and is controlled by primary processes:

"I am everything and everywhere, but at the same time everything is outside me, something other than me. Therefore I simultaneously exist as everything, move outside myself and am locked up inside myself and do not exist."

In such a world it is not at all unreasonable for the structure of objects to have a secret, living quality—a quality that the primary human environment once possessed.

In Utrillo's case the whiteness of the walls may signal his first, unsuccessful attempt to separate himself from the ubiquitous beloved and hated mother. His ambivalence between purity and impurity, between an ideal and an existence in the gutter, vanished into the empty whiteness. It became immaterial, so to speak, but still remained latent as a constantly quaking tension.

Utrillo is considered a landscape painter. But there is not much lush green vegetation in his work. Actually he is probably the first person to paint the landscapes of a big city. Sometimes he also uses a purely urban perspective, as in *Rue de la Joncquière* (1910), in which the street is viewed from above rooftops. Trees and greenery are missing. The facades of the houses are cold, dirty and grayish white. People are incidental little forms strewn around in the narrow depths of the street. Nobody knows if they're alive or not.

It seems to me that Utrillo was one of the first interpreters of environmental alienation. He was the first to know something about the phobic reactions people have to the white urban environment, which has no identity.

In many respects Graham Sutherland (born in 1903), one of the most important British painters alive today, is the direct opposite of Utrillo. He is both an artist and a law-abiding citizen. Sutherland grew up in Yorkshire and has deep roots in its landscape. Not until he reached the age of twenty-seven did he begin to discover his own style. While the uninhibited Utrillo exploded in external activity, Sutherland exercises a very rigid self-discipline, "a tortured soul and a passionate temperament beneath a seemingly tranquil appearance,"[54] as Douglas Cooper describes him in his biography.

Sutherland's work, which is governed by a tension between destructive and constructive forces, aims at a new synthesis. He portrays the phobic anxiety at abandonment and disorientation in the void, but also man's ability to structure and delineate his outer as well as his inner space. A newly integrated human being emerges from the world of objects.

Like Utrillo, Sutherland is also called a landscape painter. But in Utrillo the green vegetation is missing, and in Sutherland the landscape as an optical whole is no longer present. The romantic faith in the good, generous, healing nature, in which Freud also strongly believed, has been replaced by the skeptical, searching attitude of modern man. Sutherland doesn't believe that God created nature in order for man to find rest, new confidence and creative forces in its refuge. Nor does he think that man is the crowning glory of creation; he believes that, like all earthly phenomena, man is subject to the same inexorable laws of growth, maturity and decay. He breaks down the beautiful, harmonious whole of the landscape into a meaningless play of forms and lines. Out of this chaos he intuitively chooses a form that seems to carry a meaning just for him. In Sutherland's work this form acquires a double identity. It is both itself and an immaterial, live human figure. They form a whole and yet possess clearly distinguished separate forms and meanings. Natural formations, things created by human hands, as well as the figure of man can each speak for the other.

When Sutherland was commissioned to draw England during the Second World War, he produced pictures of burned factories, quarries blasted by bombs, machines that spit their intestines out, twisted steel, telling the tale of destruction of man's toil and trouble. When our customary means of expression no longer suffice, then *things* have to speak for human suffering, anguish and despair. In his head of Christ he combines the natural branch formation of the thornbush, twisted barbed wire—made with human hands—and pictures of prisoners in Auschwitz and Belsen.

By means of the eye's creative selectivity, man, in his psychophysical totality, rises again from the welter of form and movement. Man is Sutherland's measure and inspiration. The first human being who emerged from the chaos of our age has the same instinctive need as all of humankind: he must leave testimony of his existence. The easiest way is to build a road, a greeting to future generations. I've been here before you.

The very fact that the road exists witnesses that you can proceed along it and that another human being can be found nearby, says Sutherland. The road delivers man from emptiness and timelessness. It advances toward new goals and a new beginning of human presence.

The natural landscape appeals to man's spontaneous activity: Transform me, sow and reap me, swim in my waters, dig my earth. Build yourself a dwelling by the ocean, in the mountains, in the shade of the trees. The urban landscape makes no appeal; it is silent. The newcomer is forced to be passive. He cannot intervene and change the city. He can do many things *in* the city but nothing *with* the city. The forced passivity probably leaves a sense of alienation toward the environment that no city dweller has escaped. The neutrality and indifference of the technological environment can activate earlier phobic reactions of disorientation and abandonment in an unfamiliar, empty space where individual footsteps never leave a message: Someone has been here before you.

There is a big step from the experience of nature accentuated for generations by mankind to the unaccentuated technological environment of skyscrapers. But perhaps, despite everything, there is a path leading from the secret depths of the forest to the hidden interstices between the high-rise buildings' concrete walls:

> Raspberries betray their presence by their scent
> in the darkest wood,
> but no search will reveal
> the agonies the dead have laid aside
> and which can still quicken and tremble
> between atoms and concrete
> or there, always,
> where a place has been left
> for heartbeats.[55]

Nelly Sachs, 1967

Notes

FLIGHT AND REALITY

1. This interpretation was given by Gősta Harding.

REACHING SAFETY

1. *Regression* means going back to an earlier stage of development, and this may encounter different instances of the psychic personality. *Regression in the instincts, "Id":* from genital to pregenital instincts. *Regression in the critical observations of self,* "the superego": from social to less social to simply asocial behavior. *Regression in the ego:* permanent changes in the perception of reality. The adult's predominating objective, logical evaluation of reality fuses with prelogical, magic wishful thinking and this leads to a gradual breakdown of the normal pattern of perception, which after a while once more becomes stabilized, but now on a more primitive level.
2. R. Allers, "Ueber psychogene Störungen in sprachfremder Umgebung," *Zeitschrift für die gesamte Neurologie Psychiatrie* (1920).
3. Jean-Paul Sartre, "Literature and Communism," *Partisan Review,* Vol. 15, No. 6 (1948).
4. Otto E. Sperling, "The Interpretation of the Trauma as a Command," *Psychoanalytic Quarterly,* Vol. 19, No. 3 (1950).

5. Roheim mentions that in "Morocco the danger of being affected by the evil eye is very great while eating. To take food in the presence of some hungry looker-on is to take poison." (Geza Roheim, "The Evil Eye," *The American Imago*, Vol. 9, No. 3-4 (1952).

6. L. Richard, *Personnes déplacées* (Paris: 1947).

THE YOUNG MAN LUTHER AND PRESENT-DAY MAN

1. Erik H. Erikson, *Young Man Luther: A Study in Psychoanalysis and History* (New York: W. W. Norton and Company, 1962), p. 31.

2. *Ibid.*, p. 31.

3. Hermann Hesse, *Steppenwolf*.

4. Erikson, *op. cit.*, p. 64.

5. *Ibid.*, p. 73.

6. *Ibid.*, p. 94.

7. *Ibid.*, p. 95.

8. Sigmund Freud, *Moses and Monotheism* (New York: Vintage Books, 1967), p. 148.

9. Roland H. Bainton, *The Age of Reformation* (Princeton, N. J.: D. Van Nostrand Company, Inc., 1956), p. 96.

10. *Ibid.*, p. 26.

11. *Ibid.*, p. 25.

12. *Ibid.*, pp. 97-98.

13. Erikson, *op. cit.*, p. 115.

14. Bainton, *op. cit.*, p.97.

15. Stählin, "Cristliche Religion," in *Lexikon des Wissens* (Frankfurt am Main, 1957).

16. It seems to me that in our times another medium, namely art, is often underestimated and neglected as a means of achieving insight into one's own goals and motivation.

17. Johan Huizinga, *Erasmus* (New York: Charles Scribner's Sons, 1924), p. 207.

18. Erikson, *op. cit.*, p. 216.

19. *Ibid.*, p. 221.

20. Bainton, *op. cit.*, p. 95.

21. Huizinga, *op. cit.*, p. 207.

22. Sigmund Freud, "Why War?" in *Character and Culture* (New York: Collier Books, 1963), p. 145.

23. Bainton, *op. cit.*, p. 34.

SOCIAL CHANGE AND THE GENERATION GAP IN A CASE OF PHOBIA

1. A. Mitscherlich, "Auf dem Wege zur Vaterlosen Gesellschaft," in *Ideen zur Sozialpsychologie* (München: Piper, 1963).

2. Peter Blos, "The Concept of Acting Out in Relation to the Adolescent Process," *Journal of the American Academy of Child Psychiatry*, Vol. 2, No. 1 (January, 1963).

THE FIRST LOVE OF YOUTH—AND OF CHILDHOOD

1. The syntonic experience of the *ego ideal*: "I want to become a person like that, I wish to behave according to a pattern that suits me." There is a relation of tension between the *superego ideal* and the ego, with the superego demanding and admonishing: "That is what you will become; you must act according to a prescribed pattern." The *"personal" superego* concerns the content that has been actively acquired during adolescence, in contrast to the more traditional content that is imposed on the child in childhood. Among adults the word "conscience" implies things that are conscious. The word "superego" includes both conscious and unconscious elements and has a developmental perspective from the first signs of social behavior to the fully developed patterns of maturity. *The conscious and unconscious content* should not be confused with good and evil. Freud once said that people are not only worse than they imagine but frequently are also a good deal better than they themselves know. *Ego synton:* a feeling of authenticity that the ego never doubts.

2. *Narcissistic libido*: the ego charged with the energy of instinct (the word "libido" is disappearing from psychoanalytic theory). *Pathology*: a disturbance in the balance between the narcissistic charge (an exaggerated interest in oneself) and decreasing object cathexis (a lack of interest in other people). It is often the result of disappointment: "Since nobody loves me, I'll have to do it myself."

3. Maxwell Gitelson, "Character Synthesis: The Psychotherapeutic Problem of Adolescence," *American Journal of Orthopsychiatry*, 18:3 (1948).

4. Friedrich Schiller, *Don Carlos, Infant von Spanien*, in Vol. 3, *Gesammelte Werke* (Basel: Birhäuser, 1945).

5. Isaiah Berlin, *Chaim Weizmann* (London: Weidenfeld and Nicholson, 1958).

6. *Ibid.*

7. Learned Hand, "Democracy: Its Presumptions and Realities," in *The Spirit of Liberty, Papers and Addresses,* collected by I. Dilliard (New York: Vintage Books, 1959).

8. *Neutralized instinctual energy*: energy that has been displaced from the immediate satisfaction of clamoring physical needs, without consideration for the surroundings, to socially acceptable goals outside the child's body that demand prolonged, goal-oriented activity. *Deneutralized energy*: during periods of increased stress or semi-unconscious psychic conflicts that are difficult to resolve, the level of neutralized energy sinks and part of it flows back to the primitive original source. The ego experiences this process of the breaking down as a difficult narcissistic transgression and tries to restrain it by making a compromise: the neurotic symptom. Therefore the symptom bears witness not only to an ongoing psychopathological process but also to the ego's struggle to control this process.

9. F. Wittels, "The Ego of the Adolescent," in *Searchlights on Delinquency,* ed. Eissler (New York: International University Press, 1949).

10. *Active identification*: to act like your father, in contrast to *passive identification*: to become like your father in fantasy.

11. Gustave Flaubert, *L'Éducation sentimentale* (Paris: Gallimard, 1952).

12. Anna Freud, The Ego and the Mechanisms of Defense (London: Hogarth Press and the Institute of Psychoanalysis, 1968).

13. *Concerning the gestalt formation of the defense mechanism*: different defense mechanisms are organized into a configuration which is characteristic of the individual. As the defense mechanisms have a certain hierarchy, pathological displacements may occur in which highly developed forms yield to primitive forms of defense or are replaced by them outright. *The hierarchy of defense:* for example, if a young child defends himself against experiencing an unpleasant reality by simply denying it, this mechanism is on a lower level than the one a child uses during latency, when he tries to adjust to a difficult reality by intellectualizing and rationalizing, although this occurs at the expense of the emotional depth of feeling.

14. I have used the term "Oedipus constellation" to indicate that this basic human situation is much more varied and ambiguous than the popular concept of the Oedipus complex: the son loves his

mother and kills his father, who is his rival. As soon as we begin to discuss girls, we have a new twist. She loves her father but doesn't want to get rid of her mother. Somebody else has to do it. Perhaps Orestes, or why not Zeus himself? An inverted Oedipus constellation may sometimes follow the normal one, and the child makes a homosexual object choice with all the complications that the transformation of his own identity, among other things, implies. Sometimes a fourth person may join the basic triangle. Instead of directly approaching the one he loves, the child does it indirectly. He identifies with a person who seems to be closer to the desired parent. The child thinks that only when he has become like the other person can he be loved. The child's ability to make quick displacements occasionally leads to a situation in which he himself doesn't recognize the object of his worship or may even underestimate. A psychoanalyst who lived in Vienna tells how once when he was saying goodnight to his little daughter, she put her arms around his neck and promised to marry him when she grew up. "And what'll become of me?" her mother asked spontaneously. Suddenly the girl became thoughtful, and then she started to cry. After several days the little girl began to rave about Prince Eugene, whose statue she had passed on a walk. After a week or so she asked if she could visit her Prince Eugene again. When she came home, she spontaneously begged her father: "Dear Dad, couldn't you pose for me as a statue, like Prince Eugene?"

This anecdote also contains an element of the Oedipus constellation which is often neglected: we relinquish our love for someone because we don't want to hurt another person or lose his affection or also because we are afraid of his revenge. In other words, we are socialized, and our cooperation is the end and the heir of the Oedipal situation. Finally, I wish to point out that the concept "parents"—mother or father—is not biological. Every adult who for a long period of time takes care of a child becomes its mother or father.

15. Anny Katan, "The Role of Displacement in Agoraphobia," *International Journal of Psycho-Analysis*, Vol. 32, Part 1 (1951).

16. Heinz Hartmann, "Comments on the Psychoanalytic Theory of the Ego," *Psychoanalytical Study of the Children*, Vol. 5 (1950).

17. Heinz Hartmann, "Notes on the Theory of Sublimation," *Psychoanalytical Study of the Children*, Vol. 10 (1955).

18. *Narcissistic identification*: identification with a person who is either like oneself or—more often—has some of the qualities one would like to possess. *The pathological version*: identification with a person who despises himself or on whom one projects one's own self-contempt. *Narcissistic object choice*: the partner is chosen in the same way as in narcissistic identification.

19. *Manic defense*: a defense against a reactive depression due to a difficult, unbearable situation in life by denying the outer reality at the same time as the depressive feelings become their opposite, a slightly euphoric state of mind. *The manifest content of the defense*: "I am so happy that everyone likes me and wishes me well." *The latent content of the defense*: "I am alone and confused because people are indifferent and treat me badly." Because both inner and outer reality are tied to misinterpretations that complement each other, all the efforts at reevaluating the actual situation become more difficult, as does the adequate experience of real emotions.

MAN BETWEEN IDEAL AND INSTINCT

1. Ernest Jones, *The Life and Work of Sigmund Freud*, ed. Lionel Trilling and Steven Marcus (New York: Anchor Books, 1963).
2. Sigmund Freud, "First Lecture," in *A General Introduction to Psychoanalysis* (New York: Pocket Books, 1969), p. 22.
3. Jones, *op. cit.*, p. 343.
4. *Ibid.*, p. 322.
5. *Ibid.*, p. 67.
6. *Ibid.*, p. 127.
7. Sigmund Freud, "The Moses of Michelangelo," in *Character and Culture* (New York: Collier Books, 1963), p. 103.

PSYCHOANALYSIS AND MORALITY

1. Nils Olof Franzén, *Zola et La Joie de Vivre* (Stockholm: Stockholm Studies in History of Literature, No. 3, 1958).
2. Ernest Jones, *Sigmund Freud, Life and Work* (London: Hogarth Press, 1953).
3. Suzanne Cassirer-Bernfeld, "Freud and Archeology," *The American Imago*, 8:2 (June 1951).
4. Jones, *op. cit.*
5. Randall Jarrell, "The Obscurity of the Poet," *Partisan Review*, Vol. 18, No. 1 (1951), p. 78.

6. Victor Frankl, *From Death Camp to Existentialism* (Boston: Beacon Press, 1959).
7. William Shakespeare, *Hamlet*.
8. Vilhelm Moberg, *Nattkyparen* (Stockholm: Bonniers, 1961).
9. Karoly Kerenyi, *Autike Religion*.
10. Theodore Reik, *From Thirty Years with Freud* (New York: Farrar and Rinehart, Inc., 1940), p. 140.
11. Francis Bull, *Tretten Taler pa Grini* (Oslo: Gyldendal, 1945).

HAVE NEUROSES INCREASED?

1. Erich Fromm, "Individual and Social Origins of Neurosis," in *Personality* (London: K. Paul, Trench, Trubner & Co., Ltd., 1949).
2. Erling Eng, "Freud and the Changing Present," *Antioch Review* (Winter 1956–57).
3. Erik Goland, *Den stora ommöbleringen* (*The Great Reconstruction*) (Stockholm: Bonniers, 1955).
4. George Orwell, "Lear, Tolstoy and the Fool," in *Shooting an Elephant, and Other Essays* (London: Secker & Warburg, 1950).

A PLURALISTIC VIEW OF MAN

1. Tollak Sirnes, *Sinnets helse* (Oslo: 1965).
2. Merton M. Gill and George S. Klein, "The Structuring of Drive and Reality," *International Journal of Psycho-Analysis*, Vol. 45, Part 4, 1964.
3. Franz Alexander, *The Psychoanalysis of the Total Personality* (New York: Coolidge Foundation, 1949).
4. A. Mitscherlich, "Auf dem Wege zur Vaterlosen Gesellschaft," in *Ideen zur Sozialpsychologie* (München: Piper, 1963).
5. Erik H. Erickson, *Insight and Responsibility. Lectures on the Ethical Implications of Psychoanalytic Insight* (New York: W. W. Norton, 1964).
6. Heinz Zahrnt, "Versäumte Chancen der Kirche," in *Bestandsaufnahme* (Stuttgart: 1963).
7. August Schou, *Vatikankonsiliet* (Oslo: Norsk utrikspolitisk institut, 1965).
8. Tryggve Bull, *Aerlig talt. Frimodige ytringer om norsk politikk* (Oslo: Cappelen, 1963).
9. Karoly Kerenyi, *Ergriffenheit und Wissenschaft i Apollon* (Düsseldorf: 1953).

10. A pathological variation of this is the obsessive neurotic's sense of bondage when he is unable to free himself from a pattern of behavior that seems meaningless. Even certain religious phenoma such as dogma and ritual have obsessional characteristics.

11. Progress in psychoanalytic treatment is also experienced sometimes as grace received. The patient forgets how arduously he has struggled to gain insight that comes to him suddenly like "a gift from above."

12. C. F. MacIntyre, trans., *Rilke's Selected Poems* (California: University of California Press, 1956), p. 93.

CRISIS OF TRUST AND ALIENATION

1. Robert Coles, "Social Struggle and Weariness," *Psychiatry*, Vol. 27, No. 4 (1964), p. 310.

2. *Ibid.*

3. Viola Bernard, "Psychoanalysis and Members of Minority Groups," *Journal of the American Psychoanalytic Association*, Vol. 1, No. 2 (April 1953).

4. James Baldwin, *Nobody Knows My Name* (New York: Delta Books, 1962).

5. This account is in the first person because the illusion that everyone has an inborne ability to feel spontaneous intimacy has been a purely personal problem for me in my work as a psychoanalyst. The analysts who have not had these illusions and who in the beginning of their work were confronted by different kinds of patients have not necessarily made the same mistakes. But then they haven't had the same experiences either.

6. A term used by Dr. van de Windt, a Dutch psychoanalyst and a former concentration-camp prisoner, in an introduction to a symposium concerning the later fate of concentration-camp inmates, during the International Psycho-Analytical Congress in Amsterdam in July 1965.

7. From a Swedish newspaper article which appeared in the summer of 1945.

8. Heinz Hartmann has clearly maintained that irrational reactions need not in themselves be psychopathological. After all, there are irrational motives behind highly integrated and realistically defensive acts too. Because of Hartmann, psychoanalysis

has become a psychology of learning. We mature by finding new and more adequate solutions to conflicts that once were irrational. Or, as Arthur Koestler says, we do the right things for the wrong reasons.

9. Bengt Nerman, "Ordet som inte blir kött, Alienationen som sprakligt problem," *Kristet Forum,* 1 (1967).

10. Margaret Little, "Counter-Transference and the Patient's Response to It," *The International Journal of Psycho-Analysis,* Vol. 32, Part I (1951), p. 38.

11. Merit Hertzman-Ericson, *Svara unga ar (Difficult Years of Youth)* (Stockholm: Natur osh kultur, 1967).

12. Little, *op. cit.,* p. 39.

13. Harold F. Searles concludes his article "The Schizophrenic Individual's Experience of His World," *Psychiatry,* Vol. 30, No. 2 (May 1967), about the inner world of schizophrenics by saying that in his daily work the therapist is gradually forced to question each and every basic premise of human existence—individual as well as collective—of which he had felt so incredibly sure. "In this process we come eventually to realize that nothing about human beings and human behavior can be assumed, can be taken for granted. This has been, for me, one of the endlessly rewarding, exciting aspects of this work," he writes on page 131.

We need not have worked with chronic schizophrenics in order to come to the same conclusion as Searles, even though in my experience the positive, enriching aspect was a long process of gradual reorientation which had its moments of doubt and feelings of inadequacy.

14. Anna Freud, "The Widening Scope of Indications for Psychoanalysis," *Journal of the American Psychoanalytic Association,* Vol. II, No. 4 (October 1954), p. 607.

15. R. D. Laing, *The Divided Self* (New York: Pantheon Books, 1969).

16. Sibylle Escalone and Grace Moore Heider, in *Prediction and Outcome: A Study in Child Development* (New York: Basic Books, 1959), p. 9.

17. Erik H. Erikson, "Identity and the Life Cycle," *Psychological Issues* (May 1959).

18. See S. Kelin, "The Personal World Through Perception"; W. Dennis, "Cultural and Development Factors in Perception"; A.

Korzybski, "The Role of Language in the Perceptual Process," in *Perception, An Approach to Personality* (New York: Ronald Press Co., 1951).

19. David Shapiro, *Neurotic Styles* (New York: Basic Books, 1965), p. 177.

20. *Ibid.*, pp. 17–18.

21. The neuroses of refugees show that depersonalization as a life-supporting defense against an actual threat from the outside is quite common among people of all ages. But when the threat has disappeared the depersonalization also disappears of its own accord.

22. T. S. Eliot, "The Dry Salvages," from *Four Quartets*, in *The Collected Poems and Plays* (New York: Harcourt, Brace and Company, 1952), pp. 133–34.

23. Harold F. Searles, "Concerning the Development of an Identity," *The Psychoanalytic Review* (Winter 1966–67).

24. E. G. Schachtel, "On Alienated Concepts of Identity," *The American Journal of Psychoanalysis*, I (1962).

25. Peter H. Knapp, Sidney Lewin, Robert H. McCarter, Henry Werner, Elizabeth Zetzel, "Suitability for Psychoanalysis, A Review of One Hundred Supervised Analytic Cases," *The Psychoanalytic Quarterly*, Vol. 24, No. 4 (1960), p. 476.

26. Philip Weissman, "Sophocles' *Antigone*," in *Creativity in the Theatre, A Psychoanalytic Study* (New York: Basic Books, 1965).

27. Benjamin Wolman, "The Antigone Principle," *The American Imago*, 22:3 (Fall 1965), p. 200.

28. Karl Jaspers, *Philosophische Aufsätze* (Frankfurt am Main, Hamburg: Fischer Bücherei, 1967).

29. Friedrich Heer, *The Medieval World: Europe 1100–1350*, tr. Janet Sondheimer (New York: The New American Library, 1962).

30. With the exception of the Scandinavian countries.

31. Heer, *op. cit.*

32. Frieda Fromm-Reichmann, *Psychoanalysis and Psychotherapy. Selected Papers* (Chicago: University of Chicago Press, 1960).

33. Lars Gyllensten, *Juvenilia* (Stockholm: Bonniers, 1965).

34. Karl Marx, *Ekonomisk-filosofiska manuskript* (*Economic and Philosophical Manuscript*) (Paris, 1844); *Människans frigörelse* (*Liberation of Man*); *Ett urval ur Karl Marx skrifter* (*A*

Selection of Writings by Karl Marx), ed. S. E. Liedmann (Stockholm: 1965).

35. James Baldwin, *op. cit.*
36. Sigmund Freud, *Selbstdarstellung (Autobiography)* in *Gesammelte Werke Chronologisch Geordnet,* Vol. 14 (London: Imago Publishers, 1955).
37. I have for the most part followed Lars Roa Langlet's book *Den unge Marx og menneskets fremmedgjörelse (The Young Marx and Human Alienation)* (Oslo: 1963). It is an extraordinarily fascinating presentation of Marx's work and its social as well as philosophical background. In a convincing way the book combines an effort to be objective with a lively style, and it never loses sight of the problems of our times.
38. Arnold Ljungdal, *Marxismens varldsbild (The Philosophy of Marxism)* (Stockholm: Norstedt, 1947), but mainly his book *Georg Lukacs och marxismens estetik (George Lukacs and the Aesthetics of Marxism)* (Stockholm: Norstedt, 1967).
39. We can raise the same objection to Freud. Mental health, according to Freud, is the ability to love and to work. As far as I know he never expressed a need to be passive and rest. Nor did he believe that people could become nervous from having worked too much. Freud, like Marx, had a phenomenal, almost unlimited, capacity for work.
40. H. Kohut, "Forms and Transformation of Narcissism," *Journal of the American Psychoanalytic Association,* Vol. 14, No. 1 (1966).
41. Verbally communicated during a seminar on the psychoanalysis of blind children conducted by Dorothy Burlingham in London in 1964.
42. Pär Radström, in *Ro utan aror (Row Without Oars)* (Stockholm: Norstedt, 1961).
43. The first really systematic discussion of this was by Harold F. Searles, *The Non-Human Environment in Normal Development and in Schizophrenia* (New York: International Universities Press, 1960).
44. Jean Marie le Clézio, "En bas vers la mort" ("Deep Down Toward Death").
45. K. is the main character in Kafka's novel *The Trial.*
46. Frank Kafka, *The Trial,* tr. Willa and Edwin Muir (New York: The Modern Library, 1964), pp. 285–86.

47. Reproduced in *Konstrevy*, No. 1 (1964).

48. Fontana, Catalogue 412 of Stedelijk Museum, Amsterdam (1967).

49. *The Inner and Outer Space*, reproduced in the catalogue of the Modern Museum, Stockholm (1966).

50. *Inner and Outer Space*, relief (1964) by Lars Englund, reproduced in the catalogue of the Modern Museum, Stockholm (1966).

51. Charles Biederman, *Art as the Evolution of Visual Knowledge* (Minnesota: Red Wing, 1948).

52. Douglas Cooper, *Paul Klee* (Harmondsworth: Penguin, 1949).

53. G. Boudaille, *Le Musée Personnel* (Paris: 1965).

54. Douglas Cooper, *The Work of Graham Sutherland* (London: Percy Lund, Humphries and Company, Ltd., 1961), p. 29.

55. Nelly Sachs, "Who Knows Where the Stars Stand?" in *O the Chimneys, Selected Poems, Including the Verse Play Eli*, tr. Ruth and Mathew Mead (New York: Farrar, Straus and Giroux, 1967), p. 103.